Public Policy and Politics
Series Editors: Colin Fudge and Rob

Important shifts in the nature of public policy making are taking
place, particularly at the local level. Increasing financial pressures
on local government, the struggle to maintain public services, the
emergence of new areas of concern, such as employment and
economic development, and increasing partisanship in local politics, are all creating new strains but at the same time opening up
new possibilities.

The series is designed to provide up-to-date, comprehensive
and authoritative analyses of public policy and politics in practice.
Public policy involves the expression of explicit or implicit intentions by government which result in specific consequences for
different groups within society. It is used by power-holders to
control, regulate, influence or change our lives and therefore has
to be located within a political context. Two key themes are
stressed throughout the series. First, the books link discussion of
the substance of policy to the politics of the policy-making process.
Second, each volume aims to bridge theory and practice. The
books capture the dynamics of public policy-making but, equally
important, aim to increase understanding of practice by locating
these discussions within differing theoretical perspectives. Given
the complexity of the processes and the issues involved, there is
a strong emphasis on interdisciplinary approaches.

The series is focused on public policy and politics in contemporary Britain. It embraces not only local and central government
activity, but also central–local relations, public-sector/private-
sector relations and the role of non-government agencies. Comparisons with other advanced societies will form an integral part
of appropriate volumes. Each book presents and evaluates practice by drawing on relevant theories and applying them to both
the *substance* of policy (for example, housing, employment, local
government finance) and to the *processes* of policy development
and implementation (for example, planning, management, organisational and political bargaining).

Every effort has been made to make the books in the series as
readable and usable as possible. Our hope is that it will be of
value to all those interested in public policy and politics – whether
as students, practitioners or academics. We shall be satisfied if the
series helps in a modest way to improve understanding and debate
about public policy and politics in Britain in the 1980s and 1990s.

Public Policy and Politics
Series Editors: Colin Fudge and Robin Hambleton

Managing under Pressure

Industrial Relations in Local Government

Martin Laffin

MACMILLAN

First published 1989

Published by
MACMILLAN EDUCATION LTD
Houndsmills, Basingstoke, Hampshire RG21 2XS
and London
Companies and representatives
throughout the world

Printed in Hong Kong

British Library Cataloguing in Publication Data
Laffin, Martin, *1952–*
Managing under pressure.
1. Great Britain. Local authorities.
Industrial relations. Management
I. Title II. Series
352′.00517′0941
ISBN 0–333–44659–3 (hardcover)
ISBN 0–333–44660–7 (paperback)

For my father and my mother

Contents

Acknowledgements

I would like to thank the UK Economic and Social Research Council for funding the research on which this book is based. Thanks must also go to those people in the case study local authorities who talked to me frankly about the problems facing them and gave me access to their files. The research and writing of this book has spread over my membership of four institutions – the Tavistock Institute of Human Relations, the Policy Studies Institute and the Universities of Melbourne and Sydney – reflecting the increasingly peripatetic life-cycle of that endangered species – the British academic. I am grateful for the assistance that my present and former colleagues in these institutions have given me. I owe a particular intellectual debt to Ken Young with whom I have spent long hours discussing the recent changes in British local government. John Benson, Margaret Gardner and John Power were kind enough to comment on the earlier chapters. The series editors, Colin Fudge and Robin Hambleton, and Steven Kennedy of Macmillan have also been particularly helpful in commenting on earlier drafts.

Finally my greatest debt is to my wife, Rosa, for showing me that there is a lot more to life than writing books.

Sydney, Australia   MARTIN LAFFIN

Guide to Reading the Book

Public service industrial relations is now a major issue in many countries in Western Europe, North America and Australasia. Recent economic and political pressures have been changing the role of public sector bodies as employers. During most of the post-war period public service employers, including local authorities, have been expected by governments to be 'model employers' setting an example to the private sector in terms of employment practices. Many governments have broken with this view and are now compelling public sector organisations to be 'marketplace' employers. Accordingly changes in public service regulations and legislation have been introduced to bring market discipline into the public services by making them more dependent on raising their own finances and compelling them to put services up for outside competitive tender.

These changes in the employment role of government have given public service industrial relations greater importance. The new role presents employers, that is elected politicians and officer managers, and unions with major problems of change and adjustment. The employers are having to manage within tightened financial constraints and manage less tractable workforces and unions. Policy change, whether it be in the form of service cutbacks or of new policy initiatives, has become more difficult and public service managers are reporting increasingly difficult industrial relations problems. Meanwhile national and local union leaders are having to adjust to a new and more abrasive approach to management on the part of the employers. These problems are further compounded for employers and unions by other political and social changes.

Local government in Britain exemplifies the new pressures on public service organisations. It has been at one of the cutting edges of the radical Thatcher Conservative Government. That Government has been determined to roll back the frontiers of the state and introduce market discipline into what remains of the public sector. It has seen local authorities as cosy havens of inefficient labour market practices, employing too many people and providing employees with pay and conditions out of line with the productive economy's 'ability to pay'. Consequently local authorities have been subject to tremendous pressure both to reduce expenditure and employment levels through changes increasing their financial dependence on local rates and also to hive off to the private sector as many activities as possible.

This book is concerned with the new realities of public sector industrial relations. The book uses the example of British local government to show how managers, both elected and appointed, and union leaders are trying to cope with these new realities. The aim is to assist both practitioners and students to understand and to reflect upon the ways in which industrial relations are and can be conducted in local government and also, more widely, in the public services in Britain and similar countries.

The book introduces the major approaches and issues from academic industrial relations literature and shows how they apply to local government. More importantly the main part of the book uses two case study authorities as the starting-point for an extended analysis of the problems of managing and responding to the new realities of local authority industrial relations. The aim is to understand these new realities from the viewpoints of those actually involved in the organisation, highlighting the dilemmas and problems confronting them and their efforts to resolve them.

Thus the first set of questions addressed in this book concerns the problems of how policy makers reconcile the environmental, especially the financial, pressures on their organisation with their own policy priorities, and those pressures and priorities with the interests of their workforce.

The second set of questions arises from the new difficulties in negotiating over policy change. As management-staff relations have become more adversarial and less harmonious, managers and unionists have had to rethink their strategies to ensure the continued negotiability of change. The policy makers as managers have had to anticipate growing resistance to change which has raised questions such as: how do political leaders perceive and seek to resolve the tension between their policy priorities and good staff relations? under what circumstances do they adopt certain strategies? Meanwhile many local union leaders have had to learn how to respond to employers who intend cutting back expenditure almost regardless of the traditional local government employer concern for good industrial relations. Other union leaders have had to cope with the conflicting pressures that arise when ruling parties introduce major new policy initiatives at a time of financial stringency.

The analysis of the changing conditions of the negotiation of change is based on a typology of management strategies. Four possible strategies are indentified and explained in Chapter 2 – cooptation, collaboration, conciliation and confrontation. Recent developments are understood in terms of management shifts away from the traditional strategies of cooptation and collaboration towards the newer strategies of conciliation and confrontation. The union response to changing management pressures is understood using a similar typology of strategies and local union leaders are shown as having to rethink their strategies in similar ways to their employers.

The third set of questions arises from the highly differentiated or fragmented management characteristic of local government, that is from the blurred division of management responsibilities between elected members and senior officers. While fragmented management has always been a source of difficulties, those difficulties have been considerably increased by new economic and political pressures. On the management side increasing political instability within councils highlights the problems attached to fragmented management: who negotiates with the unions? what is the relationship between the formal and the informal channels of negotiation? On the union side fragmented management raises both opportunities and obstacles for union leaders in their negotiations with management: in what ways does differentiated management create negotiating opportunities for unions, such as through informal links with elected councillors? and in what ways can it complicate and obstruct union negotiators?

The three early chapters form a general introduction to industrial relations in local government. Chapter 1 outlines the main approaches to the study of industrial relations – the pluralist, social action, Marxist, corporatist and fiscal crisis approaches. Chapter 2 focuses on the problems facing the management side in terms of coping with environmental pressures, differentiating aspects of the managerial role and forming policies and management strategies. Chapter 3, then, deals with the unions, discussing

the reasons for their growth in local government and the recent
surge of militancy, and the problems of union leadership in a
changing economic and political climate. The chapter also places
the growth of local government union activism in historical
context, pointing to how earlier developments, such as the
incomes policies of governments previous to the Thatcher Government, have contributed towards the growth of militancy.

The next two chapters are case studies of two contrasting local
authorities selected to illustrate and to develop further the arguments about management and unions already raised in the
previous chapters. The first case study authority is Conborough –
a radical Conservative council intent on cutting back on spending
and the scope of government, a political programme which came
to include the privatisation of certain local services. The second
authority is Labton – a radical Labour council keen to implement
a major programme of policy initiatives despite tightening finances
as the Thatcher Conservative Government cut central grants and
imposed controls over the raising of local rates.

The final three chapters use the case study findings as a basis
for a wide ranging discussion of both management roles and strategies and union leadership problems and strategies.

1 Industrial Relations in Local Government

Introduction

Industrial relations in the public services has been a neglected field. Historically public service organisations have not been characterised by smouldering industrial discontent but by harmonious and well-ordered relations between employers and unions. This situation has now changed completely. In Britain 'by 1980 it had become commonplace to consider the major source of instability in British industrial relations as lying in the relationship between governments and other public sector trade unions'.[1] In a similar vein another commentator has described the British public sector unions as 'the most dynamic section of British organised labour'.[2] A similar growth in public service union militancy has been noted in other countries such as the United States and Australia.[3]

This new militancy has found expression in rising levels of industrial action and disruption in local government. In Britain over the period from the early 1970s to the middle 1980s, industrial action by local government workers has become widespread. At the national level there have been major incidents of industrial action such as the famous 'Winter of Discontent' in 1978–79 which contributed to the fall of the Callaghan Labour Government; the 1978 firemen's strike; the 1978–9 social workers strike; nation-wide action by the National and Local Government Officers Association (NALGO) in 1974 and London-wide action in 1979; and, most recently, the long teachers' action running through 1985 and 1986.

This chapter introduces the major approaches to the study of industrial relations within the public services and local government context. Five different approaches are identified.[4] Firstly the pluralist approach which sees the unions as a type of interest group and industrial relations as part of a pluralist political system.

1

Secondly the social action and Marxist approaches criticise the reformist assumptions of the pluralists and stress the function of unions as expressions of social interests rooted in deep social and economic inequalities. Thirdly, the corporatist approach maintains that these differences in social interest are capable of being regulated through the incorporation of the unions in government. Fourthly the fiscal crisis approach argues that under conditions of fiscal strain the relationship between the state and its employees is pushed into crisis as the former reduces expenditure under national and international economic pressures. The consequently worsening pay and conditions in the public services lead to employee protest and resistance, industrial relations become less consensual and the unions become channels for the expression of political disaffection and dissent.

Pluralism: the unions as interest groups

Pluralism began life as a political theory and has only recently been applied to industrial relations.[5] Broadly pluralism conceives of the political system as an arena within which there are numerous competing interest groups all involved in attempts to influence the government machine which itself is assumed to be neutral. The unions, then, are seen as one type of sectional interest in competition with others for the attention of the policy makers and for resources. Meanwhile the governmental machine itself is controlled by elected politicians belonging to that political party that has won the most votes or seats at the last election. The prime task that pluralism gives to the ruling politicians is that of balancing the differing interests and arbitrating among the various claims and demands in accordance with their party manifestos and perceptions of likely electoral consequences. An important pluralist assumption is that all interest groups have some opportunity to express their views and that no group is entirely denied access to the policy makers. It is assumed as well that interest groups usually use proper or legitimate influence channels and seldom resort to threats or sanctions against their elected rulers. For the pluralist, then, conflict can be contained within the legitimate institutions of democratic government and, indeed, should be as there is a strong normative aspect to the theory.

Pluralism has emerged as the dominant approach in the study of industrial relations. British industrial relations scholars in particular have been anxious to reject the conservative 'unitary' view of work organisations as team endeavours in which conflicts between the employer and the employed are assumed to be 'abnormal' and so either result from failed communications or the activities of outside agitators. Under this view conflict in industrial relations is defined as illegitimate. Instead the British pluralists argue that industrial conflict reflects genuine differences of interest between employer and employed and, as such, should be accepted as legitimate by management and by governments in legislating on industrial relations matters.

Indeed the pluralists portray work organisations almost as if they are governmental systems in miniature. Alan Fox, who originated the distinction between unitary and pluralist perspectives, sums up this 'governmental' view of the work organisation in quoting N. S. Ross:

> The problem of government of a plural society is not to unify, integrate or liquidate sectional groups and their special interests in the name of some over-riding corporate existence, but to control and balance the activities of constituent groups so as to provide for the maximum degree of freedom of association and action for sectional and group purposes consistent with the general interest of the society as conceived, with the support of public opinion by those responsible for its government.[6]

The problem, then, for management and union is that of how to establish and maintain adequate working relationships within the workplace despite often conflicting interests. According to the pluralists these conflicts can be and are domesticated through the creation of joint institutions such as formal bargaining procedures, grievance processes and arbitration arrangements. The field of industrial relations study, then, becomes that of the 'study of the institutions of job regulation'.[7] Similarly Bain and Clegg define the field as the 'study of all aspects of job regulation – the making and administering of the rules that regulate employment relationships – regardless of whether these are seen as being formal or informal, structured or unstructured'.[8]

The emphasis on rules is a major characteristic of pluralism in both the industrial relations and political science fields. The latter typically identify the 'rules of the game' as setting the context within which pressure groups compete for influence.[9] In both fields the underlying concern is that without rules there would be 'growing anarchy in workplace industrial relations'[10] and in society. Official support for this view of industrial relations was given in Britain by the 1968 Donovan Report which diagnosed the central problem of British industrial troubles as lying in the absence of rules and the consequent excess of informality in workplace industrial relations. [11] The Report argued that this excess of informality created a greater likelihood of disputes escalating into strikes. In particular the authors of the Report were concerned that the informal systems, which they then saw as developing in much of British industry, were undermining national level collective bargaining procedures. Accordingly the major thrust of their recommendations was that industrial relations should be reformed through the introduction of formal and agreed procedures for the regulation of collective bargaining, disputes, grievances and other industrial difficulties within industries and the individual workplace.

The dominant concern of the industrial relations pluralists and the Donovan Report has been with industrial relations in the private sector, particularly the engineering industry. The public sector and especially the public services were largely ignored by the Donovan Committee and have continued to be so by British industrial relations academics. In large measure this neglect of the public services reflects the fact that industrial disruption within those services has only recently become a matter of wide public and governmental concern. Another reason for this neglect of the public services is that they appeared to exemplify the effectiveness of the nostrums prescribed by the pluralists for the private sector. Compared with the private sector, public service industrial relations have been and still are highly formalised and institutionalised. Under the Whitley Council machinery in the public services there is a well-established national system of collective bargaining and a highly developed system of consultative machinery centering on joint consultative committees between employers and staff as well as procedures for dealing with disputes, grievances and other employment related difficulties.[12] From the pluralistic point of view, such a high degree of formalisation and institutionalisation has underlaid and made possible the stability and consensus that was until recently characteristic of public service industrial relations in Britain.

However the rapid growth of industrial unrest within the public services in Britain does raise questions about the continuing effectiveness of these institutions. The pluralist response to this unrest is to argue that there is a need to reform the institutional and technical deficiencies of the present system. For instance the 1982 Megaw Report on the pay of non-industrial civil servants recommends changes in the methods of determining public sector pay but falls back on an exhortation to both parties, especially the trade unions, to take into account market forces and other factors conducive to pay restraint in the public services.

Another response to growing public service unrest is to interpret it as actually resulting from the favoured institutional position of unions in the public sector. Accordingly the public service unions can be seen as using their institutionalised position and industrial muscle to preserve their relatively favourable employment conditions compared with those employed in the private sector. The most comprehensive critique of the public service unions in this vein is Wellington and Winter's book *Unions and the Cities*.[13] Their argument is that the unions in the public services have a privileged position compared with that of the unions in the private sector. As a result of this privileged position, they argue, the public service unions are able to short-circuit the 'normal American political process' or pluralist political process by pursuing their sectional interests through the use of essentially political sanctions not available to other pressure or interest groups. What this means is that the public sector unions enjoy such considerable advantages compared with other interest groups that the collective bargaining process is permanently skewed in the unions' favour.

The power base of the public service unions, according to Wellington and Winter, lies in their monopoly position as the sole providers of essential services and their ability to use essentially political sanctions against government. Whereas in the private sector, the degree of employer resistance to union demands is determined by market forces, in the public sector that resistance is determined by political forces. The public employer tends to put up less resistance to union demands than the private employer because the monopoly power of the unions means that the employer cannot find alternative ways of providing the services threatened by industrial action. Employer resistance, then, tends to produce widespread disruption of services that is likely, according to Wellington and Winter, to prove politically embarrassing to the elected leaders. Consequently these leaders tend to seek early and favourable settlements with the unions. This tendency is reinforced, they argue, because employers in the public sector are more sensitive to political than to budgetary factors so, to avoid a political crisis, they pass on any increases in cost in the form of higher taxation.

Another aspect of Wellington and Winter's argument is what they see as the tendency for the scope of bargaining in the public services to expand beyond those matters in which employees should legitimately have an interest. They suggest that unions too often short-circuit the pluralist democratic process by using industrial tactics to pursue political rather than industrial ends, for example unions can pressure political leaders into making decisions favouring one racial group over another.[14] So that the scope of bargaining is being widened to include issues that go far beyond just conditions of service. What Wellington and Winter are contesting is unions' rights to use the institutions of collective bargaining to pursue 'political' ends. It is an abuse of collective bargaining, in their eyes, that they see as threatening the cherished pluralist balance among interest groups.

Wellington and Winter's concerns are clearly normative. Their book amounts to a critique of collective bargaining and unionisation within the public services. They favour the closer regulation of unions and, in particular, question the extension of collective bargaining to include the public services as it would 'institutionalise the power of public employee unions in a way that would leave competing groups in the political process at a permanent and substantial disadvantage'.[15] As part of that closer regulation they also argue that strike action by public employees in the more essential public services should be made illegal.

Wellington and Winter perform an important role in highlighting the different pressures on employers in the private and public sectors. During an industrial dispute in the private sector, the employer has to balance the cost of lost revenue against the cost of any concessions that might have to be made to end the dispute. While a public sector employer has to set the 'cost of concessions' against the risk of a political crisis.[16] However Wellington and Winter assume that the public employer, the elected politicians, will almost always prefer to accept the costs of concession rather than risk a union induced political crisis. But this assumption is doubtful. Over recent years many governments in western democracies have shown resistance in the face of powerful public sector union pressures for pay increases. Clearly these governments consider the political costs of high inflation as more serious than those that might arise from industrial action, for example recent British governments have resisted union pressures.[17] Clark and Ferguson in their study of municipal responses to fiscal pressures in the US conclude:

> Widespread beliefs to the contrary, we find that organisational and political activities of municipal employees have minimal effects on general fiscal policy outputs or fiscal strain. For municipal employees to increase fiscal strain, total expenditure on personal services should increase. But most measures of municipal employee organisation or political activity are unrelated to personal service expenditure.[18]

In fact it could be argued that unions in the public services are as constrained as those in the private sector. Public service unions simply face a different set of constraints – political constraints that can be just as limiting for the unions as any market constraints. In particular the use of political sanctions is by no means a union monopoly. Contrary to Wellington and Winter's assumption, public employers can use political sanctions to constrain union action. Political leaders can and do use their access to the media during industrial disputes to put their side of the case and to undermine union support. Moreover the fact that unions can withdraw essential public services does not place them in quite as powerful a position as might at first appear. Union leaderships typically experience problems in mobilising rank and file members who have acquired commitment to a service and are consequently unwilling to take action disruptive of that service. Such commitments are far more likely to develop in the public services by their very nature than in the private sector. Politicians can and do act on this sense of commitment by condemning industrial action as 'irresponsible' or threatening to the 'public interest'.

It should be stressed that most of those in the pluralist tradition in Britain have not adopted views similar to those of Wellington and Winter. To exclude public service unions from enjoying equivalent collective bargaining rights to their private sector counterparts is anathema to most British pluralists. They argue that there are not only good normative reasons for giving unions these rights, but also strong pragmatic reasons as attempts to suppress industrial action may simply lead to other, possibly even more disruptive expressions of discontent.[19] A good example of these other consequences in Britain was the Thatcher Government's banning of trade unions in 1984 from the General Communications Headquarters which led to heavy losses of highly qualified staff.

So far the emphasis as has been on the more normative aspects of pluralist theory. The rest of this section will consider the analytical or explanatory power of pluralism. An important line of criticism of pluralism as an analytical framework has been that it is too limited in terms of the range of explanatory factors offered. In trying to explain industrial relations events, the pluralists take job regulation as the starting point which means that the main explanatory variables are sought within the employing organisation, the structure of the industry or in the role of the state in regulating industrial relations. Thus Clegg, in his major work comparing the industrial relations systems of six western countries, concludes that the main factors determining variations in industrial conflict (reflected in levels of unionisation and strike action for instance) are the structure and attitudes of employers' associations and of industrial management and the particular forms that state intervention takes.[20]

However the critics of pluralism argue that conflicts within the work organisation simply mirror wider social conflicts rather than institutional failures. Hyman, for example, maintains that the pluralists are too concerned with the consequences of industrial disputes and so overlook the sources of such disputes which lie beyond the work organisation in social and economic inequalities.[21] Goldthorpe, from a different perspective, similarly criticises what he sees as the reformist bias of the pluralists. He questions whether industrial conflicts are, as he argues the pluralists assume, soluble within present day society because 'within the existing form of society . . . a disordered state of industrial relations may be best understood not as a pathological but as a normal condition'.[22] In a similar vein Hyman, but from an avowedly Marxist position, discerns a fundamentally conservative assumption underlying the pluralists' central concern with rules and with job regulation. This conservative assumption is that the prime problem is the maintenance of order in the face of disruptive forces:

> The focus is how conflict is maintained and controlled, rather than on the processes through which disagreements and disputes are generated. From this perspective, the question whether the existing structure of ownership and control in industry is an inevitable source of conflict is dismissed as external to the study of industrial relations – which must be concerned solely with how employers, trade unions and other institutions cope with conflict.[23]

The response of those within the pluralist tradition to this type of criticism has been to make their values more explicit and to widen out their field of study. They insist that they do not seek to deny that major inequalities in wealth and power exist within society and that these inequalities ultimately form the basis of conflicts within work organisations. Nevertheless they argue that these inequalities have to be accepted as givens which form the immutable context within which unions and management have to work.[24] The pluralists accept that they have a reformist bias but point out that it is a bias that is shared by both sides in industrial relations. The unions as well as management are reformist in the sense that they prefer compromise over continuing conflict. Indeed what is remarkable is the ordered nature of most industrial relations given the profound inequities they apparently mask. Moreover Clegg stresses that to adopt a reformist bias is not necessarily to imply that the power relationship between employers and unions is one of equality.[25] Instead the pluralist assumption is simply that the workers can, to some extent, counter the power of their employers through collective organisation and action. The pluralists can also point to the problem that the social action and Marxist approaches have in trying to establish links between wider social and class conflicts and varying levels of industrial disruption.[26] The fact that work organisations in the same society exhibit markedly different levels of industrial action suggests that there are problems with the latter approaches.

More recently those in the pluralist tradition have taken over Hyman's definition of industrial relations as the study of the 'processes of control'.[27] As Purcell and Smith argue:

> Using the notion of control focuses attention not merely on the processes of rule making and application in industrial relations but on the wider area of establishing objectives and why control is necessary to achieve these objectives, the processes by which control is achieved and how effective control activities are and the limitations to the control process in goal setting, goal achievement and maintenance.[28]

This redefinition of the field is part of a trend towards a widening in the scope of industrial relations studies in Britain. There has been a break with the earlier Donovan research agenda which had a relatively limited focus on workplace and union. In contrast the recent trend has been towards a widening of the research agenda to include previously largely neglected questions such as the derivation of managerial authority and the relationship of industrial relations strategies within the workplace to corporate level management policies and strategies. This new approach will be discussed further in the next chapter on management policies and strategies within local authorities.

An important example of this new approach is Purcell's book, *Good Industrial Relations*, which builds on Fox's emphasis on the centrality of trust in industrial relations.[29] Purcell argues that mutual trust is an essential requirement for the adequate working of management-union relations. Where there is a lack of trust these relationships are 'marked by conflict and aggression with the parties essentially denying each other's legitimacy, seeking to weaken or destroy the other's organisational base'.[30] However, on the basis of four company case studies, Purcell argues that the institutionalisation of industrial relations does not automatically increase the levels of trust between management and unions; an argument contrary to the usual pluralist assumption. This argument will be taken up again in the next chapter.

Social action and Marxist approaches: the unions as expressions of social interests

Whereas the pluralist approach gives explanatory primacy to specifically industrial relations factors, the social action and the Marxist approaches give such primacy to other, wider social factors. Both approaches see the determinants of industrial behaviour as lying outside work organisations in the larger society, arguing that industrial conflicts have to be understood as manifestations of deeper conflicts rooted in basic inequities of wealth and power. The rules and institutions to which the pluralists attach so much importance are of marginal significance compared with these more basic inequalities. Indeed both the social action and the Marxist schools present these institutions as having a repressive or at least conservative function in their use as regulators of conflict.

There are important differences between the social action and the Marxist schools. The social action school detects a much greater range of interests and conflicts within society than just those of social class which the Marxists consider to be quite central. Broadly the social action model of society is that of an arena within which social actors, usually in the sense of collectivities rather than individuals, pursue their own aims according to their values and beliefs. The social action approach dismisses approaches which see actors' behaviour as determined or just heavily constrained by social or non-social forces. These approaches are regarded as ignoring the vitally important subjective meanings which people give to their actions. Instead the social action approach takes the actors' own definition of the situation in which they are engaged as an initial basis for the explanation of their actions. Individual actors are seen as both actively shaping their society and, at the same time, deriving their values from their place in that society. Consequently those within the school prefer to use the term 'action' rather than the alternative 'behaviour' which has strong positivist overtones.

The major and most influential example of this approach are the 'Affluent Worker' studies by Goldthorpe and his collaborators.[31] In their studies they emphasise the degree to which workers' 'orientations to work' are formed independently of the employing organisation but are nonetheless critical to any proper understanding of relationships within that organisation. Their sample of workers displayed a basically instrumental orientation towards their work, placing greater value on their non-work satisfactions such as family life. As a result industrial relations within the employing firm were largely shaped by the workers' single minded concern with questions of remuneration. Consequently any reorganisation of industrial relations procedures and institutions within the firm could only be of quite marginal significance given the workers' instrumental orientation.

Marxist writers have strongly criticised the social action school. Hyman, in particular, stresses what he sees as the vagueness with which that school treats those social factors to which they attach so much explanatory importance. He contends that explanations simply in terms of actor definitions and orientations are insufficient in themselves. Simply to confine explanations in social action terms is to overlook those structural influences on actors of which they themselves may be unaware: 'Definitions of social reality are themselves socially generated and sustained, and the ability of men to achieve their own goals is constrained by the objective characteristics of their situation.'[32] What Hyman is getting at is that the employment relationship is essentially a class relationship between the owners of capital and the workers, therefore, any explanation of industrial behaviour has to be located within that basic class relationship. Indeed Marxists generally argue that all significant conflicts within capitalist societies are explicable in terms of class conflict. Even though actors' own definitions of their problems at work may centre, as they usually do, on such limited matters as wanting a fair day's pay for a fair day's work, a friendly working environment and indulgent management, the Marxists argue that these definitions have to be reinterpreted in terms of the underlying class relationship. To try to explain social conflicts in terms other than class is not simply insufficient but often to propagate an ideological defence of the status quo.

There are some obvious difficulties here for Marxists. Workers' definitions of their situations in non-class terms are remarkably persistent despite, from a Marxist perspective, their 'unreal' nature. Marxists sometimes try to explain this persistence in terms of a 'false consciousness' cultivated by the employers, the media and even certain trade union leaders.[33] Undoubtedly these three influences are important in shaping worker attitudes. However what Marxists are doing is falling back on what, by their own account, are superstructural factors of the type that they criticise the social action school for using to fill an explanatory hiatus in their explanation of worker behaviour under capitalism.

A related problem for the Marxists is how to account for the unchanging reformism of the trade unions. While unions can be seen as expressions of class interest, they have failed repeatedly to realise any revolutionary potential. The unions have seldom used their collective organisation to do more than increase their influence over issues of pay and conditions, although such limited action may indirectly contribute to wider social change. In other words their aim is not to overthrow capitalist society but to win increased benefits from it. Whenever unionists have seen the pursuit of this aim as threatening the stability of society or even the future of the employing organisation they have almost invariably stepped back from the brink. In addition union organisations are typically involved in the regulation and containment of conflict in the workplace and nationally have co-operated with governments over income policies and other policies intended to shore up the existing economic system.

Many Marxists have tried to explain these instances of co-operation and collusion in terms of union leadership elites identifying their interests more closely with those of the powerful rather than those of their own members. This line of argument was given some support by the emergence of a shop steward movement in Britain during the incomes policies of the late sixties and seventies as the rank and file began to break away from what they saw as inadequate national level settlements.[34] However, although the ideology of many shop stewards appears to have exhibited some features of class consciousness in the Marxist sense, the orientations of the rank and file appear to have remained predominantly instrumental. Some Marxist commentators in the Trotskyist tradition have been quick to seize on certain disputes as indicators of an emerging class consciousness but these disputes have remained few in number as well as being open to various interpretations. More mainline Marxists in the Leninist tradition have argued that the workers' party and not the unions is the only effective instrument of working class mobilisation. But again the British Labour Party and other social democratic parties have eschewed revolutionary change and appear committed to work within the system.

Corporatism: the unions as incorporated into the power structure

The pluralist model of the political system and of the employing organisation is that of an arena within which various interest groups are competing for influence according to the accepted and legitimate 'rules of the game'. Thus the public service unions are simply another type of interest group with no special status or access to government. In contrast the corporatist model conceives of the political system as more closed and as one in which certain key social and economic interest groups, such as trade unions from the private and public sectors, have a special status and a close working relationship with government policy makers.[35] Unlike, too, the social action and Marxist approaches, the corporatist approach maintains that the organised class interests of capital and labour can and are co-operating in the long term national interest with government. These cooperative relationships are underpinned by various compromises between the unions and employers and engineered by government. The unions make gains, such as welfare state provisions, and the industrialists are given guarantees that the union leaderships will contain labour unrest. Consequently whereas pluralism implies collective bargaining over a fixed sum of possible gains between union and employer, corporatism implies a joint search for means of cooperation so that both sides may make some gains.[36]

Although the corporatist approach has been developed to apply to the political system as a whole, it can also usefully be applied to the relationship between the public service unions and their employers. Few authors have explicitly done so but the approach is implicit in many accounts of the relationship and in recent official reports such as the 1982 Megaw Report.[37] Some questions have been raised over whether the Whitley industrial relations system in the British public services is really collective bargaining in the correct sense of the term.[38] For there was a 'tacit agreement (the term social contract might have been applicable had it not been utilised for other purposes) that there was a reciprocal obligation between the government, at any level, and its employees, that so long as the government maintained its position of being a "good employer" the employees would forswear militancy'.[39] What this meant was that both sides, particularly the unions, would hold back from exerting full pressure on each other during pay negotiations in the interests of longer term cooperation. The Whitley industrial relations machinery has tended to constrain the full operation of collective bargaining and the development of full blooded trade unionism within the public services has similarly been constrained. It is perhaps only in recent years, as will be seen in the following section, that collective bargaining in a full sense has begun to emerge.

But how did corporatist relationships develop and how were they sustained for so long in Britain? Crouch argues that corporatist relationships are only possible where consensus exists, consensus making it possible to elaborate rules for the settlement of conflict, and where the employers can absorb union demands.[40] Firstly consensus has been and is easier to sustain in the public than in the private sector. The main factor is the greater ideological consensus in the public services as the conflict of interest between employer and employed is not as stark as that in the private sector. The public services are generally perceived as operating in the wider public interest and not as orientated towards the maximisation of personal profit, while the spread of professionalism and a client orientation among white collar public servants has reinforced such an orientation. Certainly the fact that the employer is also a government agency, even if not elected at least appointed by elected representatives, has given the employer considerable legitimacy in the eyes of the workforce. Such legitimacy has been further reinforced in countries like Britain where governments have traditionally adopted conciliatory attitudes towards unions. In fact the Whitley system in Britain can quite plausibly be seen, within the corporatist framework, as a means of removing public service pay negotiations away from the political sphere and so 'de-politicising' them. Contrary to Wellington and Winter's suppositions, the public unions in Britain have been unwilling until quite recently to risk confrontation with elected governments.

Secondly for corporatist arrangements to persist this consensus and union deference to government has to be underpinned by material concessions on the part of the employer. Until recently most governments in Britain recognised the importance of such concessions and maintained at least lip service to the principle of pay comparability with the private sector. Generally, too, the other benefits – job security, pensions, sickness benefits and so on – have been comparable or better than those in the private sector though, as will be seen in Chapter 3, many of these favourable conditions of public service employment are being seriously eroded under the Thatcher Conservative Government. Consequently the earlier easy consensus between unions and government as employer has been breaking down.

Before leaving the corporatist approach, it should also be pointed out that corporatist arrangements in miniature also exist within individual local authorities. Locally the consensus has been maintained through joint consultative machinery, as part of the local Whitley system, which in principle at least has provided staff with the opportunity to be more closely involved in management decisions than might otherwise be the case. The crucial question of whether these arrangements in practice amount to employer cooptation of the unions or employer collaboration with the unions will be considered in Chapter 3.

The fiscal crisis: the unions as expressions of political disaffection

The final approach to the analysis of contemporary public service unionism is that of the fiscal crisis. This approach stresses the differences in interest between state and private sector employees and how the former work in a context which breeds politicisation and radicalisation. The best known statement of this approach is that of O'Connor in his book, *The Fiscal Crisis of the State*.[41] O'Connor defines the crisis in terms of a widening gap between rising levels of public expenditure and falling government revenues. This gap is widening as, on one hand, public expenditure has grown under the pressure of rising demands for social services and for financial support to industry and, on the other, government revenues have fallen as large private corporations and workers in the corporate sector of the economy resist higher taxation. In response to this crisis and to pressures from international and domestic capital, he argues, governments have sought to cut public expenditure. These cuts have major implications for public service workers. During most of the post-war period, according to O'Connor, public service workers in most western countries, have enjoyed the benefits of economic growth. Their income levels have been comparable with those found in the large private corporations despite the inflation of the sixties and the seventies which could have been expected to have had a considerable impact on public service incomes given the labour intensive nature of the public services and their limited scope for productivity gains. According to O'Connor (arguing in a similar vein to Wellington and Winter despite their different ideological positions) the reason that public servants have been able to maintain their income levels is through the use of effective union organisation. However the very effectiveness of their union organisation is now contributing to the fiscal crisis by escalating the real cost of services and, therefore, the proportion of national resources devoted to them.

What is now happening, according to O'Connor, is that as governments search for expenditure cuts employment levels are coming under pressure and working conditions are worsening in the public services. O'Connor contends that these threats to the position of state workers are leading to their politicisation or radicalisation and the involvement of their unions on a wider range of issues than just those relating to service conditions. In particular he suggests that the impact of the fiscal crisis will lead state workers towards a recognition of their commonality of interest with client groups, the latter coming to see them as 'political equals, rather than as professionals or state bureaucrats'.[42] He goes on to speculate that alliances might be formed between the two but that such alliances would have to be based on issues relating to the quality of the service delivered and not to the remuneration of state workers which would be of little interest to client groups.[43]

However elsewhere in his book O'Connor, sharing some other Marxists' pessimism about the change potential of unions, raises doubts about the public service unions' potential to channel and cultivate the emerging radicalism within their ranks:

> even in the state sector, trade unions as such are poor instruments of radical social change because they are compelled to emphasise disciplined rank-and-file activity, tight organisational

structure, and the union shop – not political education and mass activity at the base, two important factors in the politicisation of workers.[44]

Although O'Connor's fiscal crisis thesis is based on US experience, it clearly has some relevance to the British case. However O'Connor, in common with Wellington and Winter, tends to overestimate the power of the unions. In New York, whose fiscal crisis formed the background to his argument, the municipal unions have proved unable to protect the jobs and living standards of their members.[45] Meanwhile in Britain the levels of local government employment have fallen after 1979 and pay levels have only just kept pace with those in the private sector (see Chapter 3).

There are strong and potentially radicalising influences on public service workers, but have these workers become radicalised or politicised? The new militancy that has emerged among public service workers in Britain and elsewhere over recent years lends some support to O'Connor' arguments. The British public service unions have been involved in major national campaigns against public expenditure cuts under both Labour and Conservative governments. Rhetorically, at least, they are campaigning on a much wider range of issues encompassing the quality of service provision as well as more traditional trade union concerns with levels of remuneration; a development in line with O'Connor's predictions. On the local level there has an increase in the links between the unions and local Labour Parties and community organisations. However, as will be seen in Chapter 3, where the 'proletarianisation' thesis will be discussed, these links tend to be short term and tactical in nature.

Conclusions

This chapter has highlighted certain of the strengths and weaknesses of the five approaches. The approach to the study of industrial relations in this book does not correspond closely with any one of these approaches but draws on aspects of four (the exception being the Marxist approach). It shares the reformist concerns of the pluralists with the problem of how the two sides reach and maintain mutually agreed institutional arrangements and procedures to regulate their relationship. However the approach adopted here tries to place the immediate institutional structures of industrial relations within a wider context. These structures are understood as constructs formed out of the diverse goals or purposes that actors bring to their involvement in the organisation. In this way this approach accepts the social action assumption that any analysis of social structures should begin from an understanding of the actors and their goals and, then, of how they seek to realise these goals in relation to others. Accordingly local authorities as organisations will be conceptualised as 'negotiated orders' to stress the centrality of the process of mutual adjustment, this view will be discussed further in the next chapter.

The approach in this book also breaks with the social action school by rejecting that school's tendency to overemphasise subjective beliefs formed outside the employing organisation. As Crouch observes, the social action school 'ignores a crucial aspect of human goal-seeking behaviour: the need to make constant choices about which means to adopt, or about the priority to be accorded different goals, or about the best means of treating conflicts and obstacles'.[46] Social action, then, should be seen as a 'mass of choices, each of which involves a calculation of gain and loss'.[47] So that while social beliefs are clearly important as explanatory factors, the analytically important starting point is the immediate set of choices facing actors. They make choices in terms of what objectives to pursue and what strategies to use to obtain those objectives. Accordingly in this study the key questions to be asked relate to how actors respond to the constrains and opportunities perceived within their social situations, while the main analytical concepts are those of beliefs, roles and strategies.

The last two approaches, the corporatist and the fiscal crisis, highlight the special characteristics of public service as opposed to private sector industrial relations. The former take place within the political arena where market pressures and criteria have limited relevance. As was seen their place in that arena has important implications for management and unions in terms of their choice of objectives and strategies. Post-war governments in Britain and elsewhere have shown a marked preference for stability and order in the public services even at the cost of major concessions in pay and conditions. However the fiscal crisis has made it more difficult for governments to make such concessions. In addition the post-war political consensus has begun to break up and recent governments, especially that of Mrs Thatcher in Britain, no longer share the concern of their predecessors with stability rather than expenditure.

The focus of this study will be on the process of continuing retrenchment within local government in Britain and the impact on industrial relations institutions in local authorities. The next two chapters will continue from the discussion of the basic issues in this chapter. Chapter 2 will look at the changing problems of management, pointing to the need to combine the management of internal relationships within authorities with that of external relationships with central government and the local political system. Chapter 3 will then look at the nature of unionism in the public sector, the rise of the new militancy and the problems faced by union leaders in authorities under fiscal stress.

2 Management under Pressure

The problem of management

Management remains a poorly understood and researched activity whether it be inside or outside government. The extensive management literature covering both the private and public sectors is predominantly prescriptive in nature, being concerned with the provision of practical guides for managers rather than analysing the actual behaviour of those in formal managerial positions.[1] In contrast, this study is concerned with the actual practice of management in local government and not with the formulation of prescriptions for managers. As such, the study is concerned with questions of who occupies managerial roles, how they perceive the problems posed by their organisational environment and what policies and strategies they adopt in response.

These wide concerns with management go beyond the traditional focus of British industrial relations research on the unions and relationships within the workplace. Instead, the assumption here is that industrial relations cannot be understood fully in isolation but has to be understood within the context of the broader management policies and strategies of those controlling the employing organisation. Furthermore, at least some of the major determinants of managerial behaviour have to be sought outside the confines of the immediate workplace. Even in the case of the private sector many of the decisions that have major industrial relations implications, such as those on future growth and plant closure, are not defined as industrial relations issues within firms but are taken largely independently of industrial relations considerations.[2] Similarly, Purcell observes that in the modern corporation: 'The conclusion seems unavoidable that to senior managers and corporate planners trade unions are a constraint to be dealt with at the level of operating decisions.'[3]

The historical evidence points to a similar conclusion in the case of the public sector. Studies of decision and policy making within both central and local government in Britain show that major decisions are taken within the higher reaches of government and that the industrial relations implications are left to be sorted out at the operational level. The key actors highlighted in these studies have been political parties, interest groups, bureaucratic interests and prominent personalities, while union organisations and representatives rarely figure.[4] The marginalisation of unions within British government should not necessarily be interpreted as a deliberate strategy on the part of policy makers nor as implying hostility towards the unions. In fact, the evidence until recently has pointed to favourable attitudes within government towards unions as successive governments have encouraged the unionisation of the public sector especially the development of white collar unions.[5] However, as was argued in Chapter 1, financial constraint and political change have meant that unions and industrial relations have become less peripheral concerns for policy makers with the decline of corporatist arrangement. Not only have industrial relations to be considered within the wider policy context, but in turn the management of industrial relations has become more central to policy making in central and local government.

The purpose of this chapter is to place the problems of industrial relations management within the wider policy context. It will provide an analytic account of the processes of policy making and of industrial relations within local authorities. The approach adopted, in line with the discussion in Chapter 1, is based on the notion of organisations as 'negotiated orders' within which participants are involved in a continual process of constructing, maintaining and renegotiating mutual understandings.[6] In particular, for public service policy makers or managers industrial relations will be seen as centering around the problem of how to balance their desire to realise their policy objectives against the need to maintain some basic mutual understandings that ensure the continued survival of the organisation. In other words, the central problem for the policy makers as management is how to pursue or even just maintain their own objectives without destroying the organisational means whereby those objectives can be obtained. This problem will be defined, in the course of this chapter, as that of balancing *policy* against *trust*.

The main focus of this chapter, and indeed the book, will be on this problem. The main sections of this chapter will conceptualise the problem as one of organisational control and discuss the different approaches or managerial strategies policy makers adopt in trying to resolve the problem. The first section will set the context by outlining the present structure of local government industrial relations in Britain. The next three sections will then examine these closely related questions: who are the occupants of managerial roles? What are the environmental pressures on them? And what are the organisational pressures on them?

The structure of local authority industrial relations

Collective bargaining in local governmnt is characterised by a high degree of centralisation and institutionalisation. The present system of collective bargaining is based on the Whitley Council system common to local government and the civil service in Britain. This system was introduced into local government in 1946 when the National Whitley Council created several national joint councils, the most important of which are the NJCs for Manual Workers and for Local Authority Administrative, Professional, Technical and Clerical Staff (APTC). Meanwhile, until recent legislative changes, the teachers had the Burnham Committees which were broadly similar in operation to the Whitley committees.[7] Under the Whitley system pay levels and other major conditions of service are negotiated nationally between the national representatives of local authorities and the unions.[8] Another important feature of Whitleyism is the emphasis placed on arbitration and at least until recently both sides have accepted that all disputes should be referred to arbitration.

This close, corporatist type relationship at the national level between employers and unions is replicated at regional and local levels. At the regional level there are 27 provincial councils again composed of union and local authority employer representatives. The provincial councils cover some service conditions and their joint employer-staff secretaries occasionally act as arbitrators in local disputes, the Greater London Whitley Council Joint Secretaries performed such a role in Labton during a dispute (see Chapter 5). Meanwhile individual local authorities, like Conborough and Labton, have joint consultative committees for the different groups within the workforce, typically having staff or white collar, manual and skilled workers joint consultative committees; the teachers have a comparable arrangement though they are the only producer group entitled to have representation on a council committee (the education committee). The joint consultative committees have written constitutions setting out the rights and obligations of the two sides in terms of rules of conduct and the topics for negotiations. Like their national counterparts, the local committees are composed of equal numbers of employer and employee representatives. The employer's side typically comprises elected members from the personnel committee responsible for personnel policy and senior officers from the personnel department with the chief personnel officer acting as the secretary of the employer's side. The employees' side is elected by the staff and, it should be noted, is formally at least separate from the union organisation. The employees' side also has a staff side secretary elected by the employee representatives and usually a part-time if not a full-time job in its own right. The chairs of the two sides and the two secretaries are usually important actors in negotiations which take place outside the consultative committees themselves which are too large and cumbersome to be effective negotiating forums.

Who are the managers?

It is a very useful and even essential simplification to think in terms of managers of large organisations as always acting together as if they were a single actor. Indeed, as Thurley and Wood point out, much of the conventional thinking on industrial relations assumes a managerial consensus.[9] In reality the management strata of organisations are characterised as much by diversity as by unity of purpose. The management strata of municipal councils is particularly diverse as they are more highly differentiated and fragmented than is normally the case in private sector organisations. Kochan, for example, argues that municipal collective bargaining differs so much from the conventional private sector bilateral model that it is best understood within a multilateral collective bargaining model.[10] As will be seen in the course of this book, this diversity has major implications for industrial relations. This section will consider the problems arising from the differentiation of management, particular attention being drawn to the problems posed in attaining and maintaining workable degrees of management cohesion as political changes have rendered management tasks more problematic.

There are three main lines of management diversity or differentiation – that between the political leadership and backbench councillors, between the elected politicians and the officer management and between line or departmental managers and staff managers. The first line of differentiation is one within the party group which creates problems of policy cohesion. Over the postwar period the formal meetings, the council meeting and committees, have become occasions for set-piece debates, the outcomes of which are generally determined beforehand within the party group. This political change, it has been argued, raised the level of policy cohesion within local authorities through the substitution of a disciplined and organised party caucus for a loose gathering of local representatives.[11] Even so party groups remain large gatherings in decision-making terms, typically comprising upwards of thirty councillors. Clearly the achievement of policy cohesion must still be a problem as the potential for disagreement must be considerable in such large groups. A strong political leadership can achieve the necessary cohesion through the centralisation of political power either in an individual leader or in a leadership grouping. Until recently political and economic circumstances favoured such centralisation of political power within party groups.

But serious problems of cohesion can arise where the political leadership cannot, for whatever reason, centralise power. Where political power becomes diffuse within the ruling party, problems arise in terms of achieving consistent policy making or even making policy at all and, in particular, of deciding on and holding a management line in industrial relations. Moreover the management of industrial relations is even more difficult where management negotiators lack political authority or support and more day-to-day management roles are vaguely defined and contested so that decisions and intentions are likely to be reversed.

Such problems of political leadership arising from power diffusion are now widespread in local government. Recent economic and political changes have introduced new forces making for the diffusion of power. As economic pressures have increased, competition over scarcer resources has intensified political conflict at all levels – within and between party groups and between members and officers. Furthermore political change has brought a new generation of elected member into local government, a generation better educated and more ideologically committed than the older generation and, as a result, more critical of political leaders and of senior officers.[12]

The second line of managerial differentiation is that between the elected councillors and the appointed officers. The issue of member-officer relationships is one of the most debated in the local government literature. Although constitutionally the officers are merely the servants of the elected council which is legally responsible for all the decisions made in its name, in practice the officers have a much wider role and influence. The conventional wisdom has come to be that the professional officers have effectively appropriated the real decision and policy making powers, relegating the elected members to the role of rubber-stamping officers' recommendations.[13] While this argument has often been over-stated it does reflect the fact that the earlier understandings gave chief officers and other senior officers almost exclusive responsibility for running departments and managing staff and the assurance that their exercise of managerial prerogatives would remain unchallenged by the elected members.

The political and economic developments already mentioned have disrupted these earlier understandings on the respective roles of member and officer. The elected members are asserting what they see as the increased need for political control and becoming more involved in running departments and in staff matters. The new generation of member is better educated and more ideologically committed than the older generation and, as a result, more assertive and more sceptical of professional officers. This new member assertiveness is a direct product of the new programmatic politics and tightening fiscal pressures which have led members to seek increased political control and to mistrust the commitment of the officer structure to the party programme. These developments have serious implications for chief officers and other senior officers in their mediating position between the ruling party and their own staff. On one hand they have to cope with growing demands from the party for tighter political control over the organisation, reflecting higher member expectations and tighter finances; and on the other their own staff are becoming less cooperative over policy change as financial constraints have made change more threatening for staff.

The third line of management differentiation is that between central services and departmental or local management. The service departments have traditionally enjoyed considerable independence within authorities particularly on matters of employment and industrial relations.[14] The corporate management movement in the 1970s in local government had limited success in overcoming entrenched departmentalism. But the new pressures of the 1980s have created new tensions between managers in central services and in the departments. A major area of tension has been that over industrial relations and personnel matters. As will be illustrated in Conborough and Labton the politicians are tightening their control over staffing levels and industrial relations. Accordingly the political and organisational significance of central departments has increased, including that of personnel departments. Departments like these are now increasingly involved in disputes over managerial and especially negotiating responsibility with service departments and, as will be seen in Labton, a continuing failure to differentiate clearly the responsibilities between departments can contribute to industrial relations difficulties.

Local authorities and their environments

A major part of making policy in any organisation is resolving the problem of defining the relationship between the organisation and its environment. Indeed it has been argued by some political scientists in the extreme behaviourist tradition that government policy outcomes are determined by their socio-economic environments, policy outcomes being the simply a reflection of factors such as the extent of urbanisation and the levels of taxable incomes.[15] This approach has been criticised for failing to specify how these environmental 'inputs' are actually transformed into policy 'outputs'.[16] In contrast the approach adopted in this study emphasises the problematic nature of the relationship between a governmental organisation and its environment. Organisational actors are seen as being in a continuing process of adaptation to what they perceive as the constraints and opportunities within the environment and typically engaged in internal debates over the nature of those constraints and opportunities as well as the most appropriate organisational response. Furthermore it is assumed that local authority policy makers are not only responding to environmental conditions but are also able to act themselves on that environment.[17] Thus their policies change the socio-economic environment as well as reflect changes in that environment.

Local authorities can also be seen to be occupying an inter-organisational as well as a socio-economic environment. What this means is that they are in relationships of interdependence with other organisations though the degree of dependence varies among relationships. In the rest of this section the main aspects of their inter-organisational environment will be outlined.

The central-local government relationship

The most important single relationship for any local authority is that with central government. Local authorities are limited to exercising only those powers which they have been specifically granted by Parliament, though in practice they enjoy quite considerable freedom of action within these contraints. More importantly from the industrial relations point of view, central government is able to apply considerable pressure on local government expenditures. Indeed as Newton and his collaborators observe the fiscal crisis for European local government is created by central government pressures.[18] In Britain central government is the major source of local government funding so that the government has been able to apply great pressure to local authorities by reducing their annual rate support grant (RSG) settlement. Between 1980/81 and 1983/84 the proportion of planned local government expenditure borne by rates and grants that was provided by central grants fell from 61 per cent to 52.8 per cent.[19]

Since 1980 the Thatcher Conservative Government has increased the financial pressures on local government through a new system of central grants. The new system is very complex but in brief it provides spending targets for authorities and those exceeding those targets are penalised through a loss of grant known as 'clawback'. Under more recent modifications of the system, local authorities lose more than one pound in grant for every pound that they spend above target so that any spending by an authority over the target carries a heavy financial penalty. In addition the Thatcher Government has now acquired powers to limit the extent to which individual local authorities can raise revenues locally through the rates. Under the Rates Act 1984, introducing this 'rate-capping' provision, the Government has given itself powers to fix the level of local rates in selected authorities.[20]

The other major financial constraint on local authorities is their limited control over their pay bills. Pay scales and other major conditions of service are negotiated nationally and not locally. The national level negotiating bodies, the Whitley joint national councils for each group of local government employees, agree on pay scales and other service conditions which then become binding on all local authorities. Nonetheless even within the confines of national settlements, there remains some scope for local bargaining especially over bonus or productivity schemes for blue collar workers and over the assignment of certain jobs to particular grades for white collar workers. Indeed there are wide variations in both bonus schemes and job gradings from authority to authority.

However when it comes to expenditure reductions, the national determination of pay is a constraint. Given that the wage and salary bill of a local authority represents such a high proportion of its revenue expenditure, any serious expenditure cuts must involve reductions in that bill. But as overall pay levels are fixed nationally, the only way in which an authority can reduce that bill is by reducing overall employment levels; even where there is scope for bargaining over job gradings such bargaining has tended to be an upward rather than downward process.

Recent central government intervention in local authority pay settlements has held these settlements down or at least assisted local authority negotiators to do so. Strictly central government is not directly involved in local authority pay negotiations, the Department of the Environment just has observer status at the national joint negotiating councils. But of course changes in government expenditure are bound to have major implications for local authority pay settlements given the considerable local government dependence on central grants. Since 1976 central government has introduced a policy of cash limits in fixing its expenditure, including the levels of grants to local government. Under this new policy central government no longer automatically adjusts the RSG settlement for inflation but instead only adjusts it at the start of the financial year on the government's own estimate of the probable inflation level. In this way the government has built into the RSG its view of what the level of pay settlements should be in the public sector. What has happened, then, especially under the post 1979 Conservative Government is that 'the cash limit serves as a substitute for an incomes policy'.[21]

The local political environment

Local authority policy makers have to cope not only with central government pressures but with pressures from within the local political environment. Local authorities are no longer, if they ever were, well-entrenched and powerful organisations insulated to a considerable degree from their local environments; an organisation of the type Dearlove describes in the case of Kensington and Chelsea.[22] Similarly party control in few authorities now corresponds to the model of the monolithic party tightly disciplined on parliamentary lines with whips and the use of disciplinary action against those deviating from a tightly drawn party line.[23]

Recent political change has begun a reversal of this earlier pattern of political control with its characteristic concentration of political power into leadership elites. The two party system has been disrupted by the emergence of a third party, the Liberal-Social Democratic Party Alliance. Now few councils are as electorally secure as they once were – majority parties are denied the permanent majorities they recently enjoyed in many authorities, while minority parties are more likely to gain some share in power. Local politics has become further invigorated with the development of manifestoism or programmatic politics as political parties are increasingly fighting local elections on locally devised policy platforms.[24] A related development is the growing polarisation of the two main parties as they have come to fight local as well as national elections on widely differing policy platforms. Many Conservative councils, like Conborough, have come to see their role as one of 'rolling back the frontiers of the state' and have been privatising services such as refuse collection, school meals, road maintenance and residential social work services. Meanwhile radical left-wing councils, like Labton, have been developing a new form of 'local socialism' through policies such as the area decentralisation of services, local enterprise boards, nuclear free zones and equal opportunity policies for women and ethnic minorities.[25]

Meanwhile the internal organisation of party groups within councils has become less oligarchic and party discipline more difficult to maintain as backbench councillors have become more assertive and factionalism has grown in importance. As part of the same trend the party outside the council has become more attentive to local issues and more concerned to hold councillors accountable. One reflection of this change in the Labour Party has been the enlargement of the electoral college for the council leadership and other positions to include local party representatives as well as the party group members.

As part of related political changes local community and other interest groups have become more influential than was once the case. The underlying reason for their increased influence probably lies in the decline of class loyalties so that the political parties can no longer depend on their traditional class based constituencies and have come to seek support by appealing to wider congeries of interests. In particular within the Labour Party there has been a great deal of discussion over the need to build up a 'rainbow coalition'.[26]

New types of local interest group, then, are emerging which are politically highly sophisticated and use the political parties, especially the Labour Party to win influence. Such 'entryism' is far from new and it is certainly arguable that it was pioneered within the Conservative Party by commercial and other business interests.[27] The impact on the internal political organisation of the Conservative Party of this entryism has been to create group solidarity and funds. However within Labour Groups this more recent form of entryism has fuelled tendencies towards fragmentation and political instability; Labton illustrates many of the problems that arise from political instability.

The negotiability of change under the fiscal crisis

The tasks of local political leadership have grown enormously in difficulty under the pressures of the new local politics and of a central government promoted fiscal crisis. As part of the same change political leadership and organisational management roles are more contested and so more difficult to establish and maintain. These problems of leadership and management are compounded by growing problems of organisational control. The tendency for organisational control to break down, particularly in large and complex organisations, as 'lower level participants' pursue their own interests and concerns has long been stressed by the critics of the traditional bureaucratic model of organisations. While this tendency is endemic in all large and diverse organisations like local authorities, the fiscal crisis approach suggests that it becomes more pronounced in public service organisations as the crisis deepens. Certainly the findings of this study support such a suggestion. Elected and appointed management in local authorities have faced growing resistance, overtly and covertly, from among subordinate officers. Authority and hierarchy no longer appear as compelling as they once were and there has been a widening gulf between the managers and the managed. One aspect of these developments has been the increasing contestation by subordinate officers of the policy making prerogatives of those in formal policy making roles either directly through local political channels or indirectly through simply pursuing their own goals at street level.[28]

The problem of control, then, is now a serious concern for the political leaders and senior officers in local authorities. They are experiencing growing difficulties in ensuring staff compliance with management intentions over policy and staff discipline. As was seen earlier industrial relations in local government are characterised by a high degree of structure, being highly institutionalised and formalised certainly by the standards of private industry. The local joint consultative committees, described at the start of this chapter, have crucial functions in management-staff relationships. Although most disputes are resolved outside them in less formal and more manageable settings, they are more than simply rubber stamps for decisions made elsewhere. They have significant functions in terms of filtering issues, checking and chasing progress on agreed decisions and ratifying decisions, all of which are important in the institutionalisation of conflict and, consequently in sustaining trust between the two sides.

Firstly management uses the joint committees as issue filters. The joint committees can be used as channels of information to the workforce and as organisational channels through which disputes and grievances can be brought up by the unions sooner rather than later when the chances of resolution may have declined. In addition management can use the joint committee system to reinforce the management hierarchy by insisting that disputes and grievances are dealt with at the appropriate level and in the appropriate department. Secondly the committees allow management and unions to chase progress over dispute and other types of negotiation to ensure, from their different perspectives, that the other side is not deliberately neglecting an issue. Thirdly the committees provide a formal setting within which all agreements between the two sides can be ratified, ensuring that agreements acquire the requisite authority among management and union ranks.

These institutional structures of joint committees and agreed procedures underpin the organisational order. Organisational order is a form of what Strauss and his colleagues refer to as 'negotiated order' and, as they emphasise, order within organisations is something that has to be worked at continually as it is constantly under threat of disruption as actors adjust to changes in their environment requiring them to be 'continually reconstituting the bases of concerted social action or social order'.[29] Actors, then, typically seek to reduce the inescapable uncertainties inherent in social situations by forming with each other understandings or agreements of varying degrees of explicitness in order to preserve the fragile social order. However the larger and more complex an organisation becomes, the more limited are the opportunities for actors to negotiate with each other on a face to face basis. As organisations become larger so organisational members tend to make their understandings with each other more explicit through formalising agreements and formalising joint discussions through institutions such as the joint committees. In this way the creation of institutional structures can be seen as a crucial means of sustaining conditions conducive to trust and joint working even when organisational size and complexity threaten to undermine trust.

Nevertheless, as Purcell has pointed out, the institutionalisation of the management-union relationship does not necessarily or automatically enhance mutual trust.[30] Indeed the formal constitutional structures did not always contain the growth of mistrust in either Conborough or Labton. Such structures cannot guarantee mutual trust, but they are conducive to the build up of trust between the two sides. Pre-existing relationships of trust are more sustainable if there are formal procedures to sort out potentially disruptive issues, while the construction of new relationships of trust is greatly facilitated if agreement on such structures forms part of the process of establishing trust.[31] Institutional procedures, then, create and sustain conditions for the *negotiability of change*: structure holding some aspects of a situation stable while enabling the two parties to identify areas of disagreement and use established channels to negotiate over such disagreements.

The nature of the central problem for management in local authorities should now be becoming clearer. Management has two types of broad objective – the attainment of certain *policy objectives* (reflecting changes in their values or adjustments to a changing environment) and the *maintenance of trust*. These two types of objective are not necessarily compatible. The introduction of new policy objectives is potentially disruptive of relationships and of trust and, therefore, of organisational order. Of course some policy changes may be welcomed by those in the organisation as responses to problems already perceived by them and so actually be conducive of trust and order. But other changes may be perceived less favourably by the workforce. Changes that those in the organisation see as threatening their jobs, pay and conditions, and/or their working practices are likely to provoke opposition. A competent and sensitive management will anticipate the likely degree of opposition, try to detect its origins and bargain with union representatives to reduce that opposition, and the existence of institutional structures greatly assists these activities. But some changes may be regarded as so important by management as to be seen by them as non-negotiable and they may consequently try to push such changes through despite the costs in terms of lost trust and organisational disruption. However the more usual problem for management is how to pursue policy objectives without disrupting the organisational means for their attainment. In other words, management is faced by an inescapable tension between *policy* and *trust*, between managing now and preserving the possibility of managing later.[32]

Of course this tension between policy and trust has always underlaid industrial relations in local government. What is being argued in this study is that coping with this tension is now quite central to the management task as fiscal pressures tighten. As long as growth in government expenditures continued the tension was relatively easy to resolve. The margin of extra resources that growth made available was used to accommodate change.[33] Policy change under growth typically takes the form of additional functions being attached to existing organisations while potential opposition is bought off through the upgrading of existing jobs, improved career prospects and so on, or simply circumvented through the addition of new organisational units to perform new functions. But the fiscal crisis has increased the difficulties of policy change. Now policy change tends to be more disruptive as it either means service cutbacks or resource switching in a zero-sum game as resources have to be switched from existing programmes to any new programmes in the absence of the increment of growth. In addition while policy change under growth typically involves the use of incentives, policy change under financial constraint involves the use of sanctions.

Types of management strategy

The new politics of austerity involve serious problems of policy change. The implementation of retrenchment policies encounters strong opposition from all levels of staff and their unions (as in Conborough). Even new policy initiatives involving the movement of resources rather than their reduction have often to be pushed through in the face of opposition (as in Labton). Local political leaders are finding a satisfactory balance between policy and trust more and more difficult to achieve. The concept of 'management strategy' will be used to analyse the differing approaches of political leaders to achieving a balance between policy and trust. The usage is broadly similar to what Thurley and Wood term 'industrial relations strategies' that is 'long term policies which are developed by the management of an organisation in order to

preserve or change the procedures, practices or results of industrial relations activities over time'.[34]

There are four main strategies available to the policy makers
as management. As has already been seen, incorporation or *cooptation* has been the traditional strategy with management trying to
minimise the differences between the unions and themselves by
absorbing the unions into the management structure and
persuading union officials to accept the management definition of
the rules of the game. In this way management has endeavoured
to avert possible challenges. The reverse of cooptation is *collaboration* where the management is giving primacy to the interests of
the union and is willing to bend the rules of the game in favour
of the unions. However as fiscal pressures have tightened on local
authorities, management has tended to move towards a collective
bargaining strategy more typical of private industry. This strategy
of *conciliation*, then, combines a recognition of the legitimate role
of unions as partners in bargaining with an emphasis on trust. At
the same time conciliation is by no means untinged by antagonism
towards the unions as management may well drive a hard bargain
with the unions while remaining basically conciliatory. Finally
management may decide on a strategy of *confrontation* to impose
their will on the unions, a strategy that implies a rejection of the
legitimate role of the unions in bargaining and thus risks
destroying even the possibility of trust between the two sides.

(1) Cooptation

Cooptation has been the traditional, corporatist management
strategy in British local government and particularly so in the case
of white collar staff. Selznick defines 'cooptation' as 'the process
of absorbing new elements into the leadership or policy-determing
structure of an organisation as a means of averting threats to its
stability or existence'.[35] Management absorbs or incorporates the
union leadership into the management structure by persuading
them that both they and the employing authority share the same
interests and the same definition of their problems. Thus conflict
is domesticated through influencing the attitudes of local union
lay officials and rank and file unionists, the strategy typically being
presented to the unions as an invitation to participate in joint

problem solving. Management can then use union 'participation' to lower union expectations and avoid overt conflict.

The choice of cooptation, as with any management strategy, reflects the dominant ideological assumptions of the controlling party. In many Conservative authorities cooptation is associated with a paternalistic attitude towards staff especially where squire-archical social elites remain dominant. In contrast in many Labour authorities cooptation arises from assumptions of fraternity rather than of paternalism. Councillors in Labour authorities tend to assume that their unions should automatically support their employers on the basis of their ideological affinities as the two branches of the Labour Movement. These councillors can point to their political programmes and argue that the unions should be supporting such socialist policies. Accordingly they expect the unions to be very cooperative and flexible over any changes in service conditions involved in implementing such policies. For reasons which will be discussed in the course of this book, these expectations are often disappointed and can serve to complicate the management of industrial relations. Certainly in those authorities of a radical cast, like Labton, there has been a growing member resentment of what is seen as obstructionism from the unions to policy change.

Clearly the strategy of cooptation remains workable only for as long as the union leadership and rank and file continue to identify their interests fairly closely with those of management. As retrenchment begins to affect pay and conditions, the continuing feasibility of the strategy is increasingly questioned. For such corporatist arrangements to succeed, as has already been noted, requires that some material concessions should be forthcoming from the employer. Consequently cooptation has been increasingly replaced by conciliation as the main management strategy.

(2) Collaboration

For obvious reasons collaboration is limited to Labour authorities as the possibility of collaboration arises from the organisational and ideological affinities between the Labour Party and the unions. All the non-teaching unions with the important exception of NALGO are affiliated to the Labour party both at national and local levels and as such send delegates to the constituency and district (local council level) parties. Traditionally collaboration took the form of informal meetings and deals between councillors and union officials but such informal arrangements were limited to the manual and craft unions and did not extend to the white collar unions. Nowadays these organisational links or affinities are strengthened by the growing involvement of local union members in the Labour Party in their personal capacities. Given these affinities collaboration can be seen as a response by some Labour leaders to the wider problems of managing the political environment as well as to the narrower problems of industrial relations: the collaborative approach reflects a need to cope with and defuse possible challenges from the local Labour Party as much as a need to cope with the industrial relations problems within the council organisation.

Again ideological as well as organisational affinities are conducive to collaboration. As a strategy collaboration offers Labour councillors one way of resolving the identity crisis inherent in their role as employers – while ideologically they identify with the unions and the employed, their role as elected representatives means that they have to act as employers in implementing their policy programme. These problems of identity are further compounded where this programme commits them to giving the unions a more participative role in management.

But Labour authorities have been moving away from collaboration as union demands have come to be seen as jeopardising the attainment of the local party programme. Many ruling Labour Groups have found that despite the organisational and ideological affinities, unions have tended to see new policy initiatives in a pragmatic light as opportunities to win enhanced service conditions. Under conditions of financial restraint even Labour councils have only a very limited capacity to accede to union demands so that the introduction of major policy changes, like decentralisation, is likely to generate tensions between councillors and unions.

(3) Conciliation

Cooptation and collaboration have declined as significant strategies with tightening financial pressures on local government. As has already been indicated there is a trend towards the substitution of corporatist arrangements within local authorities with collective bargaining type arrangements. Managements adopting a conciliatory strategy accept the basic legitimacy of the unions as partners in negotiation over service conditions and work practices. In consequence the institutional structures of joint committees and agreed procedures have grown in importance and become more formalised as authorities have turned to conciliation and away from cooptation or collaboration. These institutional structures are important because they serve to contain any disruptive conflict that may emerge as the two sides recognise divergence in rather than identity of their mutual interests. Nevertheless that institutional structure reflects the underlying balance of power between the two sides and is therefore not neutral in its effect on the balance of power.

An important aspect of conciliation is the scope of bargaining, that is the range of issues that both sides accept as legitimate matters for management-union negotiation. There is not necessarily any automatic agreement over what should or should not fall within the scope of bargaining. In particular political leaders may well refuse to negotiate with the unions over any matters relating directly to their policy programme. Both Conservative and Labour councillors have a strong sense of their electoral mandate and consequent right to fix policy, as will be seen in Conborough and Labton. Moreover political leaders have to consider more pragmatic 'management' type reasons for controlling and limiting the extent of union participation (these reasons will be considered in Chapter 6).

(4) Confrontation

Confrontation represents an extreme rejection of the earlier period of corporatist understandings. As yet it is not a widespread strategy in local government despite the Thatcher Government's increasing resort to confrontation with public service unions (see Chapter 3). It is one response to the environmental pressures of declining resources and to resistance among staff and unions to service retrenchment. Where the latter are seen as obstructing retrenchment, whether overtly or incidentally, the elected members may conclude that the most appropriate response is to challenge the unions and weaken them. Confrontation, too,

typically reflects the ideological predispositions of the members
and so is usually more than simply a pragmatic response to a
situation.

Typically confrontation involves breaking either formally
agreed rules or less formal understandings. The employer may
break these rules of the game to impose an 'agreement' unilaterally by simply refusing to negotiate over its terms. Such a refusal
usually involves an attempt to call the union's bluff in the belief
that local union leaders will be unable to mobilise their members
over the issue. Otherwise management can set out to weaken the
position of the union less directly by setting out to change the
rules of the game in its favour, challenging past union gains as
expressed in locally agreed consultative procedures. Such action
can be the prelude to further challenges on substantive matters,
it usually being easier for an employer to fight over procedural
than substantive issues given the difficulties unions have in
mobilising their membership over procedural issues. Alternatively
such action may be simply one step towards removing union privi-
leges as an end in itself.

Management, too, can deliberately ride out industrial action in
order to bring a union to heel, the Conborough dustmen's strike
being a good example. Local authority managements, as was
noted in the last chapter, are in a good position to ride out such
action because the elected members' personal financial situation
is very seldom at stake and because strikes in the public sector
usually save money for the employer. Nevertheless the members
still have to consider the possible electoral consequences of industrial action. Unions can use such action to embarrass the ruling
party politically, while management can use their claim to an
electoral mandate to justify imposing their will on the unions.
Moreover the timing of elections can be significant in influencing
the behaviour of participants as will be seen in the cases of both
Conborough and Labton. Where there is the possibility of a
change in political control, the unions may delay negotiations in
the hope that the incoming council will prove more amenable to
their demands. In contrast a ruling party anticipating electoral
defeat may decide to confront the unions to force through their
policies prior to the election.

Conclusion

This chapter has looked at the current problems of industrial relations from the policy makers' or managers' point of view. These problems have been placed within the context of the new challenges facing local authority policy makers as a result of recent political and economic change. The major environmental pressures on authorities have come from a central government tightening of the financial screws through reductions in central grant, the introduction of a penalty system on 'overspending' authorities and, more recently, of rate-capping. The increasing polarisation of British politics has further contributed to the worsening of central-local government relations especially where a Conservative central government and Labour local authorities have come to confront each other.

Meanwhile at the local level a new generation of local politicians has come to power. Generally they have a more ideological view of the world and a greater commitment to policy change than the previous generation of local councillors. Yet paradoxically the problems of change within local authorities have never been greater. As will be seen in the course of the book these problems arise in the course of both policies of retrenchment and of policy innovation. Thus the search for a middle course between the attainment of policy change and the maintenance of trust with the workforce and unions has never been so difficult for policy makers. The two case studies of Conborough and Labton have been selected to highlight these problems of policy change and the search for trust within two contrasting authorities. One is a radical, Thatcherite Conservative authority intent on reducing expenditure and the role of the local state. While the other is a radical, left-wing Labour authority intent on introducing some measure of local socialism through new initiatives in areas such as service delivery, local economic development and equal opportunities.

3 Unions under Pressure

The growth of unionism

Why do workers combine together to form unions? A wide diversity of answers have been offered in response to this question. The pluralists generally offer lists of factors such as employer recognition or dissatisfaction with income levels to explain union membership, while the social action and Marxist approaches generally interpret union membership as expressions of interests formed primarily outside the workplace. Both approaches provide some important insights into the reasons for union growth yet fail to bridge that vital gap between collective action and the subjective meaning of individual action (as was argued in Chapter 1). In this context Crouch's concept of 'usefulness' is an important bridging concept.[1]

In terms of rational self-interest there would seem to be little incentive for individual workers to join the union or participate in collective action. Individuals can remain passively outside the union yet still receive any benefits arising from collective organisation and action within their workplace. Membership of and participation in a union costs time and money yet the efforts of one individual are unlikely to have much impact on the outcome of pay bargaining: individuals can enjoy the benefits of union organisation without incurring the costs of membership.

One means of giving individuals a good reason to join a union is to provide selective benefits that are dependent on membership and so exclude 'free riders' from enjoying the benefits of membership.[2] Indeed unions do typically provide benefits such as insurance, shopping discounts and, more importantly, legal support and representation for members threatened with disciplinary action or sacking. But the provision of such selective benefits does not adequately explain union membership. Such benefits only constitute a minor incentive for membership as they represent a small return on the individual's investment of time and money. Moreover it would be difficult to explain the much

42

greater union density in the public compared with the private sector as a function just of varying levels of selective benefits. Thus the provision of selective benefits falls short of being a full explanation of the spread of union membership and particularly individual involvement in industrial action.

Explanations, then, of the growth of unionism simply in terms of narrow self-interest have limited plausibility. Crouch proposes an explanation in terms of the perceived 'usefulness' of union membership, a broader conception of rational self-interest. According to Crouch the growth of union membership depends on the extent to which workers perceive the 'usefulness' to themselves of union organisation. He argues that the prime advantage of union organisation is that it offers employees the ability to resist the power of the employer. This advantage has to be achieved collectively as only collective efforts are likely to bring employers to the negotiating table or to affect significantly the outcomes of such negotiations. Consequently union membership can be seen as varying according to workers' perceptions of the usefulness of that membership. This notion of 'usefulness' has two aspects. Firstly workers have to see themselves as *dependent* on unionism, seeing it as having major advantages over other forms of individual or collective action. Secondly workers have to experience a reasonable *ease* of union membership and organisation if they are to combine in unions.

Firstly employees are dependent on unionism insofar as there are no alternative means of improving pay and conditions either on an individual or a collective level. Those workers who enjoy good prospects for individual advancement or promotion are less likely to perceive union membership as advantageous than those lacking such prospects. Similarly those who have alternative means of collective advancement, usually in the form of professionalism, find few advantages in unionism. Thus white collar workers, who typically enjoy good career prospects and are often organised into professional associations, have traditionally had low rates of union membership. This favourable situation has now begun to change. As their employing organisations have grown in scale, many white collar workers are finding that their opportunities for individual advancement have become more limited and their relationships with their employer less personal and more rule-bound. As white collar work has become bureaucratised so the former have resorted to unionism which was previously seen as an exclusively blue collar mode of collective action. Incidentally the resultingly rapid growth of white collar unionism indicates the weakness of arguments that status boundaries have impeded the growth of unionism among white collar employees.

Secondly union growth requires some ease of membership or at least a relative absence of obstacles to membership. Workers concentrated in one place are more likely to recognise common interests and to perceive a need for collective representation and action than more dispersed workers. Union membership is typically high in large, unified workplaces, such as are found in the public sector, which facilitate contact and union mobilisation. Levels of union membership are also affected by the attitudes of the employers, union membership being greater where employers encourage unionism than where employers are hostile towards unions. Moreover union membership is particularly high where employers have accepted institutionalised collective bargaining as union organisation appears more useful to employees. Thus high levels of unionisation are found in public services around the world as governments tend to encourage rather than discourage union membership, an important exception being the United States where government bodies have often been hostile towards unions, for example in all but eight of the states public service strikes are illegal.[3] In contrast the favourable attitude of successive governments in Britain has encouraged unionisation, union membership being higher among both blue and white collar workers in the public than in the private sector.

Conversely the lack of ease of union membership can help explain the failure of some groups of workers to resort to union organisation despite having apparently strong grounds for discontent and high dependence on unionism. Their workplaces may be geographically dispersed, distance between workers limiting contact and mobilisation, or they may be divided into different occupational groupings. Another important obstacle may be the activities of employers in resisting unionisation by threatening sanctions against union members or through conceding material benefits to their employees in an attempt to reduce the attractiveness of union membership. Such counter-strategies to unionisation have often been used within the private sector to discourage union membership. It is only recently in Britain under the Thatcher Conservative Government that such counter-strategies to 'deprivilege' the public service have come to be used within the public sector.[4] In line with its rejection of the consensual politics dominant in post-war Britain, the Thatcher Government has broken with the earlier, more co-operative approach in favour of a strongly confrontationist approach to management in government and the rest of the public sector (an approach illustrated by the study of Conborough in Chapter 5).

The growth of unionism in local government

Having sketched out the main reasons behind the growth of unions, the discussion can now turn to the more specific question of union growth in British local government. As was seen at the beginning of the chapter, local government in Britain is characterised by a high level of unionisation. Bain and Price give an overall estimate of local government unionisation of just over 77 per cent in 1979 and Ingham gives figures for 1982 of 77 per cent for white collar and 70 per cent for manual workers.[5] These are overall figures and so obscure wide variations between authorities in levels of union membership, thus levels of manual unionism range from a low of 24 per cent to a high of 100 per cent while levels of white collar unionism vary from 29 per cent to 100 per cent.[6] As will be seen in this section the reasons for this high level of unionisation can be understood in terms of dependency and ease of membership.

There are five major unions and a host of other unions representing the local government workforce in Britain. The three main manual or blue collar unions are the National Union of Public Employees (NUPE); the General, Municipal, Boilermakers and Allied Trades Union (GMBATU); and the Transport and General Workers Union (TGWU). NUPE is exclusively a public service union and has members in the health service, the water industry and other public services as well as in local government. About 38 per cent of local government manual workers belong to the Union. In contrast the bulk of the members of the two general unions is found outside local government in industry and the rest of the public sector. Moreover taken together the local government membership of these two unions is less than that of NUPE with 16 per cent of local government manuals belonging to GMBATU and 11 per cent of local government manuals belonging to TGWU.[7]

The white collar staff, unlike the manual workers, are concentrated into a single Union, the National and Local Government Officers Association (NALGO) which boasts a membership level of 72 per cent among white collar staff. In contrast the teachers are spread over more than one union. There is about the same level of unionisation among schoolteachers: roughly half of the unionised teachers belong to the National Union of Teachers (NUT), another quarter to the National Association of Schoolmasters/Union of Women Teachers (NAS/UWT), just over 15 per cent to the Assistant Masters and Mistresses Association and just less than 10 per cent to the non-union Professional Association of Teachers (PAT).[8] Finally teachers and lecturers in the local government higher and further education sector are organised into the National Association of Teachers in Higher and Further Education (NATHFE).

The other and smallest group of local government workers is the craft workers (except the uniformed services of fire and police with which this book is not concerned). These are drawn from a wide range of unions in particular the Union of Construction and Allied Trades and Technicians (UCATT) and the Electrical, Engineering, Plumbing and Allied Trades Union (EEPTU). For obvious reasons these workers are concentrated in direct works and maintenance departments. Unlike the other groups of workers, the craft workers are more mobile between local government and the private sector so are less dependent on local authorities for work. Nevertheless they can be significant actors on the local scene especially in Labour authorities as the craft unions often have very close relationships with the Labour Party as will be seen in Labton.

Surprisingly the oldest union in local government is a white collar union, the National Union of Teachers (NUT). The emergence of the NUT is a good illustration of how the creation of the new public services, as the welfare state developed, gave rise to large numbers of employees with a sense of shared interest. In the case of the NUT the expansion of the public education sector, following Forster's Education Act of 1870, led to a rapid growth in the numbers of teachers employed. The early NUT inclined towards a professional rather than trade union model of collective action, the main objective being to improve the labour market position of the individual member. Thus the major Union goal was the establishment of a teachers' registration council to improve their market position through controlling entry and qualifications. Even so the teachers did develop a strong sense of opposition to the local school boards as employers, a sense that was not attenuated by the involvement of management (as in the case of local government administrative staff). Nevertheless they eschewed industrial action as a tactic and instead focussed their attention on central government – lobbying Parliament, sending deputations to the Department of Education and other pressure group type activities.[9]

The foundation of the white collar National and Local Government Officers' Association (NALGO) took place thirty-five years after the NUT in 1905. Its emergence reflected the development of a group consciousness comparable to that of the teachers. Significantly the foundation and early growth of the Association did not take place against the background of particularly unfavourable employment conditions. Local government officers at the time enjoyed better than average salary levels, job security and career prospects than their equivalents in the railways or in manufacturing industry.[10] Another unusual feature of the Association's foundation was that the founders were drawn from the ranks of senior employees and managers; an important contrast, too, with the NUT. Not surprisingly their blueprint for collective action was taken from the professions and not the trade unions. As the then NALGO General Secretary observed in 1910: 'Anything savouring of trade unionism is nausea to the local government officer and his Association.'[11] Thus NALGO's formation was characterised less by economic discontent than by a desire to create a national local government market for their skills by removing barriers to career movement between local authorities. Accordingly its early goals stressed enhanced professionalism, the education and training of members, a national superannuation scheme and the attainment of national pay sales across local government, while the Association did not adopt any procedure for calling industrial action until the 1960s.

NALGO did not begin to acquire full trade union functions

until after the Second World War.[12] Indeed until very recently NALGO has continued to correspond to Prandy's characterisation of public sector white collar unions as 'less protest bodies than administrative unions' whose funtion is 'not so much to challenge the system as to make it work more effectively by providing for the representation of staff opinions and reactions.'[13] It has even been suggested that the existence of the NALGO organisation within local authorities provided senior managers with a channel of influence over their subordinates complementary to rather than in opposition to their use of bureaucratic authority.[14] At the same time NALGO, together with the more specialist local government professional associations, also had an important function as a countervailing force to that of the local politicians. For its formation did reflect a certain sense of the opposition of interests between officers and local politicians as employers. Notably the first attempt to introduce Whitleyism into local government after the First World War was lost through the opposition of individual local authorities.[15]

The first manual unions in British local government were founded over twenty years after the NUT. Unlike the NUT and NALGO there has been little organisational continuity between the original unions and their present day successor unions. The forerunners of the manual unions were formed in the last two decades of the nineteenth century. Among the first was the National Union of Gasworkers and General Workers founded in 1889 and the Municipal Employees Association founded in 1899, both of which amalgamated in 1924 to form the National Union of General and Municipal Workers now the General, Municipal, Boilermakers' and Allied Trades Union (GMBATU).[16] Similarly the Workers' Union, which had many local authority members, was founded in 1898 and was absorbed into the Transport and General Workers' Union in 1929.[17]

The emergence of these unions, as with NUT and NALGO, followed the creation of large scale workplaces. The newly built gasworks and tramway depots formed especially fertile breeding grounds for the new unions. Unlike the two white collar unions these new manual unions were not limited to the local government or the public sector. Indeed their emergence in local government was due more to factors common to both the private and public sectors rather than specific to the public sector or local government. Nonetheless early on union activists recognised the tactical advantages of using political channels to achieve industrial ends. At the turn of the century, as Clegg and his colleagues note: 'the attitude of local authorities to trade unionism varied greatly from one area to another; but, where the unions managed to build up some political strength, they could exert an influence which was not available in private employment'.[18] For example by 1893 the Gasworkers had 'placed 18 men and women upon the various Municipal Councils, School and Local Boards, also Boards of Guardians'.[19]

British local government, then, provided favourable conditions for the initial emergence of white and blue collar unions. Central government and local authorities (more tardily) gave early recognition to the unions. The attempted establishment of Whitleyism in local government in 1919, largely as a result of growing trade union pressures as servicemen returned from the War, gave a limited boost to unionisation in local government and the public sector. But growing employer acceptance was no protection against economic recession and the late twenties and early thirties were times of setback for the manual unions in both local government as well as in the rest of the economy. Memberships slumped, forcing amalgamations of the smaller manual unions.[20] In sharp contrast NALGO's membership actually rose over the same period. But despite having registered as a trade union in 1920, under the threat of heavy membership losses, the Association retained its staff association stance.[21] Its opposition to proposed government expenditure cuts during the thirties was accordingly muted compared with today.[22]

The corporatist relationship between central and local government and the public sector unions was inaugurated under the national Whitley system for pay determination in 1946. The Whitley system reflected the consensual politics of the post-war political settlement in Britain and accordingly incorporated a consensual view of management-staff relationships. As part of this settlement post-war governments have been at least as concerned with stability and order within the public services as with their cost. In particular public employers were seen as 'model employers'. Thus the 1946 Charter, under which the system was introduced, stated that local authorities should endeavour to be in the 'first flight of good employers'.[23] Under this Charter the

National Whitley Council created several national joint councils, such as those for Manual Staff and for Local Authority Administrative, Professional, Technical and Clerical Staff (APTC).[24] Since then pay levels and other main conditions of service for manual and APTC staff have been negotiated at the national level between the national representatives of local authorities and the unions.[25]

The growth of militancy

Since the mid-sixties there has been an increase in militancy among white and blue collar workers in local government (and in the rest of the public services).[26] In particular the white collar unions have moved closer to a trade union model and away from the earlier professional model of collective representation and action. From the late 1960s onwards their strategies changed considerably with TUC membership and the growing use of industrial action. NALGO joined the TUC in 1964 after years of internal debate and the NUT followed four years later.[27] NALGO finally adopted a strike procedure in 1961 though the first official strike (involving just eighteen members) did not take place until 1970.[28] However the NUT used national industrial action before NALGO during the 1967 teachers' pay dispute.[29] Since then the use of industrial action by white collar and by manual staff has become common.

The roots of this militancy lay in a new and powerful sense of discontent among public sector workers in Britain. Unions and workers in local government, in common with other public sector workers have developed a strong sense that their living standards have worsened compared with their equivalents in the private sector. The evidence of recent shifts in pay lends some support to this view. Over the last fifteen years prior to 1985 there has been a definite downward movement in local government pay relative to the private sector. This downward movement has taken the form of a cyclical pattern as local government workers have lagged behind other workers for a time and then caught up with them after a pay review. This cyclical pattern reflects the differential impact of sucessive government incomes policies on private and public sector pay. For obvious reasons during incomes policies governments have had more success in imposing their guidelines in the public than in the private sectors. But while governments have shown themselves able successfully to depress public service incomes during such policies, they have subsequently come under pressure to introduce a catching up exercise for local government and other public sector workers. As Winchester observes, 'a similar cycle of relative pay decline, increasing conflict and large pay awards seem to have occurred and contributed to the outcome of a general election in 1979 and 1974'.[30]

This cyclical pattern can be discerned in the pay of all three main groups of local government employees between 1970 and 1985: the manual, teaching and APTC staff. Manual workers' earnings, prior to 1970, were well below the national average. The 1970 Scamp enquiry partly closed the gap between them and the national average but during the 1970s the gap again widened as the result of the Heath Conservative and Wilson/Callaghan Labour Governments' pay restraint policies. The subsequent upsurge of discontent culminated in the 1978–79 'Winter of Discontent'. The Clegg comparability exercise then brought local government manual earnings closer to the national average. This settlement was actually implemented by the Thatcher Conservative Government as a result of an election promise to honour any Clegg recommendations (a notable recognition of the significance of the public sector vote). However more recently the Thatcher Government has let manual earnings once again slip downward in absolute and relative terms.

White collar pay has followed a similar cyclical pattern. The pay of local government administrative, professional, technical and clerical (APTC) staff remained broadly in line with the national average for white collar workers until 1977 after which it began to fall behind as the result of government policies favouring the lower paid in the public sector. The 1979–80 comparability award, following national level industrial action by NALGO, improved their position as did the 1980 arbitration award. Since then there has been a steady fall in earnings compared with the national white collar workers average. Similarly teachers had slipped behind white collar average earnings until the 1975 Houghton award. Their relative pay was then again eroded until the 1979 Clegg award and the 1980 award arising from the Thatcher election promise. Since then there has been a steady fall in their relative pay despite their long and drawn out industrial action.[31]

Of course pay restraint in the public sector is just one consequence of the fiscal crisis, other serious material consequences are job losses and worsening working conditions. On job losses manual workers have been the most affected group of workers in local government with a fall in the numbers employed over the last ten years (up to 1986) of over 25 per cent.[32] Similarly the numbers of teachers and lecturers have fallen by 7 per cent between 1979, the highpoint in their numbers, and 1986. In contrast the numbers of full-time non-manual workers, excluding teachers, have actually increased over the same period by just under 5 per cent.[33]

These differences in the changes in overall employment levels among the main groups of workers in local government reflect several factors. Manual employment has been particularly severely hit by privatisation and by cutbacks in expenditure on capital and maintenance projects. Privatisation has barely touched the white collar workers, though there have been significant reductions in the numbers of jobs in engineering and architecture arising from the large reductions in capital expenditure. Meanwhile employment levels in the personal services of social services and housing increased considerably during the late seventies and since then have been maintained. It is also important to note that changes in employment levels have varied widely from authority to authority, for example Conborough reduced its employment level by over 25 per cent between 1979 and 1986, while Labton actually increased employment by more than 10 per cent over the same period.

Clearly the threat as much as the reality of job loss can create discontent among the workforce. Certainly in an authority like Conborough widespread anxiety among the workforce over the future of their jobs contributed to their willingness to take action. Even in an authority like Labton, with a good record in terms of employment growth, the industrial unrest there in part reflected widespread anxiety among staff over their future employment.

Another important implication of employment changes has been the consequent limitation on career expectations for staff. Given that careers are mostly the prerogative of officer staff, these limitations have affected them more than blue collar staff. Until

the late 1970s officer staff had very favourable promotion prospects as local government continued to expand at a substantial
rate. But the considerable slowing down in the rate of growth of
white collar jobs has meant a similar slow down in promotion
prospects. Whereas total employment over the seven years before
1986 increased by just over 4 per cent, prior to 1975 the average
annual increase was about 4 per cent.[34] Such a marked change in
employment growth has involved major changes from earlier
career expectations within local government. Those officers who
joined during the years of rapid growth and high expectations are
particularly likely to have a strong sense of discontent. As the
paths of individual advancement are closed off, so workers' dependency on unionism increases, for they are more likely to see union
activism as a means of compensating through collective action for
what they can no longer gain through individual action.

So far the discussion has been limited to the impact of changes
in the material or extrinsic rewards from work. These changes
are clearly of great importance but there has also been growing
discontent with changing intrinsic rewards from work. Over recent
years these rewards have been eroded through worsening work
conditions, growing workloads, inadequate resources and,
perhaps most importantly, increased management control over
employees.

In the context of the declining intrinsic rewards from work, it
will be recalled from Chapter 1 that O'Connor argues that public
service workers are being subjected to a process of 'proletarianisation' as a result of pressures arising from the fiscal crisis.[35] A
major feature of this process is a loss of control by workers
over their own work. Thus Braverman, in the most developed
statement of the proletarianisation thesis, maintains that skilled
workers are being 'de-skilled' as their work is being fragmented
into a series of limited tasks allowing the individual workers less
and less control over their work. In Braverman's terms there is a
growing separation of the 'conception' of work from its 'execution'
as employers increase managerial control under pressures arising
from changes in the capitalist mode of production.[36]

Although most manual workers in local government are
'unskilled', the thesis still has some relevance to manual workers.
As has just been seen their material or 'objective' conditions have
worsened significantly in relation to other workers, while they

have been subject to increased control by their local authority employers. In particular there has been a spreading use of incentive bonus schemes by the employers as they seek to contain costs.[37] The consequence of such schemes has been to reduce employee control over their work. The proletarianisation thesis has more relevance to white collar employees. It has been argued that these workers are being proletarianised as their work situation and, therefore, interests are coming closer to those of the working class. Oppenheimer, for example, argues that professionals are being proletarianised as they lose their work autonomy and become increasingly subject to control within large-scale bureaucracies.[38] Within these bureaucracies, according to Oppenheimer, hierarchical control is intensified by the administrative elites through the increased codification of professional work, a process which is made possible by the highly specialised division of labour characteristic of modern organisations.

In sharp contrast to the proletarianisation thesis, there is the 'post-industrial society' thesis. According to this thesis highly educated white collar workers, especially professional workers, form a 'new class' whose power lies in the possession of knowledge and expertise.[39] The possession of 'cultural capital' by members of this new class enables them to act independently of other power groupings within society, in particular the owners of capital. Eliot Freidson, for example, sees society in future as increasingly dominated by the professions, that is institutionalised expertise, rather than generalist management. In Freidson's view, professionals are able to resist the rationalising trends of large bureaucracies and to use their claims to special expertise to capture major positions of authority within those bureaucracies.[40] Much of the writing on British local government adopts similar technocratic assumptions about the influence of senior professional officers, often being strongly critical of this influence.[41]

Both the proletarianisation and the post-industrial theses are very general arguments about the dominant direction of change in work organisations. A study such as this is not the place to discuss whether or not there is one single or dominant direction of change in society. However some conclusions can be drawn in relation to local government. As was seen in Chapter 2, the ascendancy of the professions in local government has been eroded by recent political and economic changes. Among the top officers there is certainly a wide consensus over what they see as a loss of influence and an erosion of their salary levels over recent years.[42] This sense of discontent has also expressed itself through a search for a new form of collective representation for senior management officers and, if anything, this search has represented an increasing sense of separation from rather than identity with other workers. At the national level the formation of the new management union, the Federation of Unions of Managerial and Professional Officers (FUMPO), reflects many top officers' view that NALGO has ceased to represent their interests and instead has concentrated on representing the interests of low level officers (who, of course, comprise the great majority of NALGO members). This discontent with NALGO culminated in the overwhelming vote by chief officers in 1984 to replace the NALGO representatives on the Chief Officers' Joint Negotiating Committee with FUMPO representatives. It would seem that chief officers themselves are seeing unionism as a significant means of defence.

Of course the growing identity problems of the senior managers support rather than weaken the proletarianisation argument. These problems suggest that more junior officers are being treated even less as colleagues and more as bureaucratic subordinates. Moreover discontent has also been spreading among rank and file professional and other white collar staff. Although it is difficult to obtain hard empirical evidence on the state of officer morale, the view is widespread within local government that there are serious problems of declining morale.[43] Top-down pressures have intensified on all white collar officers both directly from financial cutbacks and from the uncertainties generated by the continuing climate of threatened cutbacks. The professional officers are experiencing the greatest changes in the sense that they are facing severe discrepancies between their expectations, and past experience, of their jobs and the present and changing realities of those jobs. In particular the white collar 'street level bureaucrats' who are actually delivering the services to the public are finding it more difficult than ever to reconcile the demands of the service consumers with the resource constraints of their organisations.[44]

The other major contention of the proletarianisation thesis is that the deterioration in incomes and job conditions is conducive to the development of a working class consciousness among white collar and professional workers. In other words that the new militancy also equals a new radicalisation as O'Connor argues in his fiscal crisis approach. Insofar as the hallmark of working class consciousness could be said to be union membership and activism, increased industrial action lends some support to the thesis.

A number of other developments also appear to support the thesis. Since the mid seventies the internal structure of many NALGO branches has been decentralised and democratised mainly through the introduction of shop steward systems similar to those found in the blue collar unions. These changes took place in the NALGO Branches in both Conborough and Labton. Although central branch negotiation remains in the hands of the officials, there is more workplace negotiation and the maintenance of support among the shop stewards and rank and file members has become more critical. Other important developments potentially indicative of working class identity are the increasing cooperation between NALGO branches and the manual unions (for example in Conborough) and the growing involvement of NALGO members, though not the Union organisation, in local Labour Parties. Meanwhile NALGO officials, as will be seen in the case studies, are increasingly disposed to use the rhetoric of class struggle.

Nevertheless serious doubts must exist over whether the new militancy is really symptomatic of a new working class consciousness among white collar workers. An adequate explanation of the new militancy is quite possible in terms of their increased dependency on union organisation without reference to a new class consciousness. Indeed the new militancy could even be seen as an attempt to prevent proletarianisation and, more specifically, as a response to manual union organisation and shrinking differentials with the manual workers.[45] The declining career prospects facing white collar workers are also important. Their dependency on unionism has increased as financial restraint has limited their opportunities for individual advancement particularly as professionalism, that traditional white collar means of collective advancement, has come to seem less relevant or useful as its anticipated rewards – career advancement and work autonomy – have been eroded.

Another reason for the new militancy among white collar officers lies in their market situation. White collar officers usually have skills that are specific to the local government sector and not easily transferred outside that sector; social work, housing management, environmental health, planning and so forth being predominantly local government occupations. So that, in Hirschman's terms, in response to the pressures just described unless they remain 'loyal' or shut up, they have to resort to 'voice' or protest within their authority as 'exit' from local government would most probably mean a considerable fall in income.[46] Consequently the union organisation becomes the main expression of voice. At the same time the use of voice has few costs for these staff. In contrast for most blue collar workers exit has fewer costs as they tend to be unskilled or have skills, especially craft workers, which are not specific to the local government sector.

Despite 'new class' type arguments, local authority white collar unionism has been predominantly defensive, being concerned with protecting existing gains rather than winning new gains from the employer.[47] Thus links with manual unions, local Labour Parties and consumer groups can be seen as tactical rather than ideological in character. This is not to say that ideology has no relevance. Clearly some local NALGO leaders derive their motivation from their ideological commitments, identifying their struggle with that of the working class. However the evidence indicates that these commitments are formed *outside* rather than *within* the work organisation. In their study of local government white collar unionists, Nicholson and his colleagues refer to 'educated radicals' for whom political socialisation supplied the 'origins for the greater part of the motivational energy for members' need for involvement [in the Union], with parental values and educational induction providing the means for people to acquire beliefs about their relations with the union'.[48] It seems very likely, too, that educated radicals have concentrated themselves in local government and the public services, particularly in inner urban authorities, rather than in private sector employment.

In any case these educated radicals remain a small minority. While they may be able to obtain election to office, once in office their ability to pursue ideological commitments is severely constrained by the necessity of getting the support of their more conservatively minded members. The NALGO leaders in both Labton and Conborough who could be described, indeed described themselves, as 'educated radicals', reported such constraints on their freedom to pursue other than limited union objectives.

Union structure

At the national level the local government unions are highly centralised. This centralised structure reflects the highly central-ised bargaining system in local government in which national officials negotiate over pay and major service conditions. These national officials have considerable power although, in common with other unions, constitutionally the annual conference is the main policy making forum. Generally the unions have a three tier structure of national, district and branch level organisation. Again, as with other unions, the local government unions have experienced some decentralisation of bargaining over recent years. The manual unions have taken the lead in decentralisation. The larger general union, TGWU, was the first to encourage the introduction of a shop steward system within the workplace though it was soon followed by NUPE and GMBATU. NUPE in particular saw a very rapid growth in shop steward organisation in the mid-1970s.[49] A major factor in this increase in lay member involvement was the introduction of local productivity bargaining.[50] For the first time local lay officials had to take decisions on service conditions and negotiate with local employers over productivity bonuses.

NALGO followed the lead of the manual unions in the late seventies. Local branches were encouraged to introduce shop steward systems in place of the traditional system of departmental representatives.[51] Under the traditional corporatist system small groups of branch officers had conducted joint decision-making with management, so that the involvement of rank and file members was minimal. Now in many branches, such as Conbor-ough and Labton, that system has been replaced by shop steward systems akin to the workplace representation and bargaining systems typical of industrial blue collar unionism in Britain.[52]

At the same time the role of the full time official in the local government unions has changed. District officials are now more involved in local negotiations though there are variations in their levels of involvement. For example the full time NUPE officials were much more involved in local negotiations in both Conborough and Labton than were their NALGO counterparts, reflecting the better educated lay officials found in the latter. Obviously, too, less experienced branch leaderships are more likely to look to full-time officials for assistance than more experienced leaderships.

The relationship with the employer

The first sections of this chapter have set the context of industrial relations within individual local authorities. It has been argued that the new militancy has arisen from the basic conditions of growing discontent and a growing sense of dependency on union organisation, especially among white collar workers. While these factors affect workers in all authorities and so help to explain the overall trend towards increased union activism, they do not explain the particular form that relations take in individual authorities. The wide variations in management-staff relations across authorities, in part at least, reflect differences in the ways in which individual actors have adjusted to their particular circumstances. As was argued in the last chapter the actions of the policy makers as managers should not be seen as determined by their environment but rather as responses to environmental pressures. In other words managers have some scope to define their roles and chose their strategies in relation to changing political and economic pressures. Similarly local union leaders are not simply products of their members' discontent but are able to channel and direct that discontent. Like their employers they have some scope to define their leadership roles and choose their strategies within the constraints imposed by the wider environmental factors and their own memberships' willingness to continue to support them. The rest of this chapter will outline the problems faced by local union leaders in managing both the external relationship with their employers and the internal relationships among their own members.

The power structure of the local union organisation is by no means independent of the power structure on the management side. A centralised management power structure tends to produce a similar pattern on the union side. The union side has to be able to field authoritative negotiators to match those whom the management is putting forward. Accordingly the former tend to acquire considerable formal and informal authority within the union. Similarly a decentralised management structure encourages decentralisation on the union side. When the management side is unable to field authoritative negotiators, any advantages the union side may derive from having authoritative negotiators acting on its behalf are lost. Moreover the presence of factions within the ruling party encourages activists other than the formal leaders to open up their own points of negotiation.

The fragmented nature of local authority management has other implications for union leadership. Some appreciation of the changing currents of thinking within the ruling party can be useful for union leaders preparing bargaining strategies. While the division between appointed and elected management poses a further complication as union leaders have to decide at what level to negotiate over what issues.

Conditions of low trust pose serious problems for both unions and management. A low trust relationship is one of purely economic exchange where the workers and their union are suspicious of every move by management and insist on bargaining over every matter of the least significance. Under these conditions union representatives try to tie management down to explicit agreements and to prevent management from taking any independent decisions. Typically both sides come to recognise that they each have more to gain from at least antagonistic cooperation than from perpetual conflict. Both managers and local union leaders have a strong mutual interest in reducing uncertainty and conflict through the institutionalisation of agreements and channels of consultation and negotiation. In other words both sides have a shared interest in creating and maintaining conditions conducive to mutual trust.

In addition institutionalisation is an important means of limiting management control over the workforce and extending union influence. Unions are enabled to formalise gains made through negotiation and so limit employer encroachment on existing areas of worker autonomy. Of course the greater the degree of trust, the more likely unions and workers are to agree to co-operate over change. Some changes are not threatening and may be seen as enhancing working conditions and even worker autonomy. Other changes may be perceived as threatening and as extensions of managerial control and, therefore, to be resisted. To prevent such extensions occurring, union representatives typically demand a right to be consulted over any changes relating to work practices.

Thus the distinction between the *process* of change and the *outcome* of change is important. Workers may agree with or acquiesce in the intended outcome of a proposed change but still insist on the right to consent to or be consulted in the process of change. From the union point of view the danger of accepting a proposed change without going through agreed procedures is that the employer may take this as a precedent for pushing through less desirable change. In any case employer initiated change under austerity conditions is often viewed as creating opportunities for winning concessions.

The increased incidence of industrial disruption suggests that the negotiability of change has become more problematic. The union side is experiencing a problem comparable to that faced by management caught in the tension between policy and trust. For local union leaders the problem is one of finding a balance between too much collaboration and too much confrontation.If they are too forthcoming in negotiations,they risk being absorbed by the management or overthrown by a membership revolt or both; if they are to adamant in their claims, they risk the total disruption of their relationship with management or the alienation of their own members or both.[53] Thus the search for a balance between the two has implications both for the relationship with the employer and the internal management of the local union organisation. This search can be further understood in terms of four union strategies comparable with those available to the management side: collaboration, cooptation, confrontation and conciliation:

(1) Collaboration

Collaboration is the traditional strategy of the local government unions, especially NALGO. It refers to the corporatist situation in which the local union organisation is virtually incorporated into the management structure and the leadership accept the employers' definition of the situation. In other words, from the employer's point of view it is cooptation. Collaboration has become less and less viable as a strategy largely because of the factors mentioned earlier which have reduced the earlier tendency of workers to identify with their local authority employer and have produced a more adversarial relationship between employer and employed. Even where the union leadership and rank and file favour the idea of joint working, unless trust is almost absolute they have to consider the possibility that they are simply being manipulated by the management.

(2) Cooptation

The other main traditional strategy used by unions is that of cooptation of the management. From the management point of view it constitutes collaboration with the unions and rests on the willingness of the elected managers to sympathise with the unions and share the latters' assumptions. The strategy arises exclusively in Labour authorities where the organisational and ideological affinities present within the Labour Movement create the opportunities for cooptation. For the most part, it would seem, cooptation existed as an indulgency pattern on the part of management mainly towards the manual workers, for example through not policing too closely the work practices of groups like the refuse collectors. Recent financial pressures have considerably reduced the willingness of authorities to continue with these indulgency patterns.

(3) Conciliation

It has already been noted that unionists have come to see the Whitley machinery less as a forum for 'joint problem solving' and more as a means for institutionalising antagonistic cooperation. They have come to recognise the potential for self-protection in these institutions. In any case under the new realities of industrial relations union leaders are finding that conciliation has become the only feasible strategy. Nevertheless it should be stressed that even within a conciliatory strategy, the leaders still have to find and maintain a balance between the extremes of collaboration and confrontation.

(4) Confrontation

Confrontation refers to a strategy adopted by a local union and not just to a situation of industrial action. Almost invariably it is seen by the union leaders and their members as a protective rather than offensive strategy, industrial action or threats of action are now even less rarely used in pursuit of union initiatives. In the context of service cutbacks confrontation means a refusal to cooperate with or participate in consultations over cuts. It is a high risk strategy as failure is likely to involve the employer implementing cuts without making any of the concessions that might have been extracted through a less adversarial approach.

To be successful or effective industrial action has to involve groups of workers who both occupy *strategic locations* in the employing organisation and have low *substitutability*. The better the strategic location of the workers, the greater will be their ability to impose heavy costs on the employer through the withdrawal of their labour or through non-cooperation. For example the withdrawal of cashiers or those managing the short term funding in an authority is often an effective tactic. However the advantages of strategic locations will be lost if the strikers have a high degree of substitutability.[54] In other words the easier it is for employers to replace workers, the less likely the strike will be to succeed. For example unskilled workers can occupy a strategic location yet the effectiveness of their strike action is reduced by the relative ease with which they can be replaced by other workers, such as happened in the case of the Conborough dustmen.

Leadership in local union organisations

Union leaders have to concern themselves with leading their own local organisation as well as with management relations. The role of union leader is well described in C. Wright Mills' phrase as a 'manager of discontent' who 'organises discontent and then sits on it'.[55] Discontent has to be stimulated and articulated yet expressions of discontent have also to be controlled if the leadership is going to be able to negotiate meaningfully with the employer. Threats of industrial action are pointless unless the union leaders are confident that they can carry them through and that they can control any action that might take place. Thus the managers of discontent have to be sensitive to shifting opinions among the rank and file and be able to focus discontent. Expressions of discontent are also used tactically in the relationship with the employer to convince the latter that the union leaders are actually holding the workers back from even more extreme action.[56]

The need to search for a middle path between too much confrontation and too much collaboration also has implications for leadership. The search produces factions within the local union organisation both at leadership and membership levels, factional divisions reflecting both ideological differences and differences in how the employer is perceived.

Insofar as the introduction of shop steward systems and the greater emphasis on rank-and-file participation has diffused power within the union organisation, the task of union leadership has been considerably complicated. This task is further complicated by divisions within the workplace and work organisation. The presence within local authorities of several unions representing different groups of workers has given rise to significant divisions within the workforce. In many local authorities these inter-union tensions have seriously impeded the attainment of a common front among the workforce. Even in Conbrough where privatisation posed a common threat there were serious problems in achieving and maintaining joint action.

There have also been minor demarcation disputes between unions. The three main manual unions have white collar sections and some disaffected NALGO members have joined these sections. For example some officers opposed to the 1984 strike by NALGO in Labton left that Union and joined the GMBATU officers section. Although the latter 'poached' only a handful of members, relations between the two unions locally were seriously affected.

The more major source of difficulties lies in relationships between blue and white collar workers. Tensions between the two groups arise from a generalised sense of resentment among the former with the latter's apparently better pay and conditions of work and from specific conflicts arising from the supervisory relationship between the two types of worker. Blue collar workers tend to identify white collar workers with management so that resentments relating to management become focused on the white collar supervisers. Particularly as authorities have sought savings through revised productivity and bonus schemes, white collar managers have come to be associated with a tightening of managerial control. Once this association takes place, joint action across the blue and white collar unions becomes more difficult.

Another significant source of difficulties, particularly for NALGO, arises from internal union divisions. NALGO is unusual in being a 'vertical union' encompassing all levels of employee from chief officer down to junior clerk. Indeed historically, as was noted earlier, the Union was dominated by senior rather than junior employees, participation in the Union being seen as conducive rather than as detrimental to career advancement.[57] Although the present generation of NALGO leadership is composed of less senior officers than was previously the case. The interests of the various groups of NALGO members, especially those of senior and junior staff, do not always coincide as the emergence of FUMPO, the new senior officers' union, testifies. As management-staff relations become more adversarial, senior management officers come under increasingly conflicting pressures from the Union and from council members as their employers. In terms of the management of discontent this hierarchical division means that senior officers are much less willing to join industrial action than their junior colleagues, resulting in a consequent weakening of Union solidarity.

Another aspect of the power base of local union leaders is their membership of the wider union beyond the boundaries of their employing authority. The unions have national policies and guidelines passed by their national conferences which are, in principle, binding on local officials. Since the late seventies the main local government unions have had national policies of opposition to expenditure cutbacks in the public services. In particular these policies reject negotiations with employers over reductions in the total numbers of jobs. NALGO and NUPE have taken the lead in national campaigns against cutbacks from 1976 onwards, NALGO especially has spent large sums on anti-cutback publicity, for example the Union spent one million pounds on a national campaign in 1983. Both unions are also strongly opposed to the increased use of outside consultants and agency staff by authorities instead of appointing permanent staff. In the education sector the NUT has played a similarly leading role. The national conferences of these unions have taken the view that the overall level of employment in the public services should not be permitted to fall. Local branches of these unions have also been called on by their national conferences to conduct local campaigns against cuts and to liaise with service user groups, such as council tenants and parents, and with other unions and the local Labour Parties.

The wider union offers the leaders of the local union organisation the possibility of extra support as well as guidelines for action. But they are also involved in problems of centre-periphery relations. The centre or headquarters of a union is reluctant to commit the union nationally to a local dispute as the risk of an even partial surrender of control is seen as considerable by the national leadership. The potential costs of national involvement in terms of strike pay and union credibility could be large yet the benefits for the union nationally are likely to be small. These problems of centre-periphery relations are well illustrated in the case of Conborough where the local union officials received only limited assistance from their national unions.

More importantly local union officials, in taking a lead from the national policies of their unions, often face problems in devising strategies consonant with these policies given their particular local circumstances. Recent policies have implied a strategy of resistance in the form of total non-cooperation with any employing authority proposing cutbacks in existing employment levels. In practice local union organisations, particularly manual and craft unions, have come under pressure to take a less principled and more pragmatic stance.

Conclusion

Historically unionism developed in local government through a recognition of shared concerns and interests among workers. Major factors in the growth of the unions were the favourable conditions for association and combination provided by large scale workplaces. Further ease of membership was ensured by the absence, for the most part, of an actively hostile view of unionism within central and local government. Moreover, in the case of

NALGO, membership was legitimised among other grades of staff through the leading role played by senior officers in the Association. Nevertheless, given their then low level of discontent compared with other groups of white collar workers, white collar officers would very probably have been deterred from membership had a hostile or unfavourable view of unionism been adopted by either central or local government. Union recognition through the Whitley System, then, was not a major factor in initial union formation, though it may be more important in ensuring the continuing relevance of unionism to members. At the same time there was a weak sense of conflict of interests between employer and employees. In particular the formation of white collar unionism was characterised less by economic discontent than by a desire to create a national local government market for their skills by removing barriers to career movement between local authorities.

More recently increased fiscal pressures have brought a new militancy to the local government unions. Discontent has spread as local government workers have seen their relative living standards worsen in relation to other groups of workers. Indeed a strong case could be made out that governments have themselves contributed towards the radicalisation or politicisation of the local government workforce by holding public sector pay down and only conceding more favourable settlements in the face of industrial pressures. Under these pressures local government unionism has become increasingly defensive in character as workers have sought to defend their jobs and living standards.

The problems of union leadership have grown in parallel to the new militancy. The central problem confronting union leaders is that of finding a balance between too much confrontation and too much collaboration. If they are too confrontationist they risk total defeat by the employers either through alienating their own rank and file or through an inability to mount effective industrial action, while if they are too collaborationist they risk a membership revolt or being swallowed by the employer. As was noted these problems of finding a middle way are complicated by the growing diffusion of power within local union organisations. These problems will be illustrated in the next two chapters on Conborough and Labton and analysed in greater detail in Chapter 7.

4 Radical Conservatism and the Unions

Introduction

When the Conservatives took control of Conborough from Labour in May 1978, after seven years in opposition, the political climate both within the country and within the Conservative Party was changing radically. Although Labour was still in power nationally, central government had been urging local authorities to hold down spending since 1975 and there was a growing sense that the years of continuing growth in the public services were drawing to a close. Meanwhile within the Conservative Party a major ideological shift was in progress. The new Leader of the Party, Margaret Thatcher, was already explicitly rejecting the post-war political consensus, making it clear that the Conservatives when and if they took office would reverse the social democratic trend of government. The aim of this new brand of Conservatism was 'to roll back the frontiers of the state' and apply 'marketplace' discipline to public service employers.

This changed political climate is important in understanding the Conservative approach to government in Conborough. There was a significant influx of new and more radical councillors into the Conservative Group and many leading members consciously saw themselves as conducting an experiment in radical conservatism. Even some older and more established members of the Group sympathised with this view, though within two years both the Leader and the Deputy Leader had resigned to be replaced by members from the new intake of younger politicians. The Conservatives were eager to get results quickly as it seemed quite possible that their period of office would be only four years as 1978 had been a good year electorally for them. This sense of a constrained horizon gave the Conservatives a new sense of urgency and determination to clear out the Augean stables of socialism.

On industrial relations the Conservatives did anticipate some resistance from the unions. At this stage they saw the manual unions as being potentially the most difficult to reconcile to the new administration. There had been almost ten years of industrial unrest in the refuse collection and street cleansing departments under the former Labour administration. On the white collar staff, the conservatives envisaged major cuts in their numbers but did not anticipate the extent to which the NALGO Branch would resist such cuts.

The political leadership: 1978–1985

Over the first seven years of Conservative rule there were three leaders and two deputy leaders in Conborough. The first Leader resigned to become mayor after one year. He was succeeded by a politically ambitious younger councillor who remained Leader during the most difficult period of industrial strife. When he left after the 1982 elections to enter national politics, he was succeeded by another younger councillor who continued his predecessor's style of abrasive leadership. Almost as important was the Deputy Leadership which was linked with the key Chair of the Finance Sub-Committee as well as that of the Personnel Committee, both of which were held by the two successive Deputy Leaders, except for a short period when the Personnel Chair was held by a less influential councillor. The first Deputy Leader and Personnel Chair was one of the older generation of Conservatives and, as will be seen, his more conciliatory and independent negotiating approach was particularly important in securing the early staff reductions against union resistance. He left in May 1981 to take his turn in the mayoral chair. His replacement as Personnel Chair could not wield the same political influence within the Group necessary for effective negotiations on sensitive industrial relations issues, as will be seen, and neither did he have the personal qualities of decisiveness and initiative required. In May 1982 he was replaced by the then Deputy Leader.

It is important to note that in Conservative groups, unlike Labour groups, only the Leader is directly elected and other positions are appointments by the Leader. Thus the Leader is a powerful figure as he or she controls patronage.

In Conborough the Leader, the Deputy Leader and two or three other chairs formed an inner caucus which became intimately involved in the running of the Council. Early on regular, fortnightly meetings were established between the Leader and his key colleagues and the Chief Executive and his Deputy. Other chief officers were occasionally invited to these meetings but even where their own services were discussed they were not necessarily invited to attend, a source of some annoyance for several chief officers. From early 1980 a 'Staff Review Team' was set up to deal with staffing levels, monitor all new posts and act as the steering group for departmental reviews and reorganisations. Again the Team was highly centralised, consisting of the Chief Executive, the Director of Administration, the Deputy Head of Personnel and the Personnel chair. The Team proved to be a critical instrument in the Conservatives' management of the retrenchment process in Conborough.

The departure of the chief executive

The existence of the Staff Review Team as a joint member-officer group reflected the Conservatives' view that they had to become closely involved in the management of the Council to achieve their aims. Their leadership quickly came to believe that they were confronting strong bureaucratic resistance to change, certainly stronger than that encountered during their earlier period of office after 1968:

> In 1968 if I had gone into a department and said, 'I want to cut back that department and keep those services going' to the Director, he would do it and I didn't have to monitor it very much. In 1978 that was not the case. We had to have much more active member involvement in it but, even given that one did work fairly closely with the directors as to what they thought should be done, we had to actually do it ourselves and monitor it ourselves.

Broadly the chief officers had come to accept continuing growth as the norm and saw themselves as service developers, whereas the Conservatives were intent on retrenchment which inevitably meant reversing service officers' expectations. Within a few months of the Conservatives assuming office strains began to appear between them and the then Chief Executive. The latter had been appointed by the previous Labour Administration to manage an essentially growth-orientated situation. Personally he would seem not to have welcomed the prospect of retrenchment and was not seen as having the toughness that the Conservatives believed was essential.

The problem for the Conservative leadership was how to replace the Chief Executive with the minimum of political and industrial relations damage: 'There was a feeling that we would be pilloried if we sacked the Chief Executive within a short time of coming into power so this held us back'. They were reluctant to be seen as setting a precedent, in terms of politicising the post. A second consideration was the memory, still very fresh in the Leader's mind, of the bitter battle that had occurred over the sacking of an earlier chief executive in Conborough (it should be added for very different reasons). A third consideration was the likely impact on officer morale in the authority as it would undoubtedly be seen as an attack on the principle of job security in the authority by the unions and staff. Sacking the chief executive could prove of tremendous symbolic importance among staff already wary of Conservative intentions.

The Conservatives decided to demote rather than sack the Chief Executive. Immediately the Labour Opposition condemned this move as a politically inspired victimisation of the Chief Executive and stated that they would not participate in the appointment of his successor. NALGO joined this condemnation but were in a slightly difficult position as their member affected, the Chief Executive himself, had apparently decided not to appeal against his demotion. The Conservatives were in a cleft stick. They could not easily defend their decision without appearing to scapegoat the Chief Executive:

> The issue had been arranged on the wrong grounds. It is much easier to fight the truth or even half the truth but when you are fighting something that is completely missing the point, it is very difficult without being brutally frank and clear about the reasons.

The situation was only finally resolved when the now former Chief Executive left to take up another job. After his departure the Conservatives decided not to appoint an outsider to the post at least partly because of the fear of further problems. Instead they asked the other chief officers to apply for the job but, in the event, only the Director of Finance applied and he was given the job. Significantly he was only appointed on a three year contract though, as he was within four years of retirement, it made little difference. It was during his term of office that the close relationship between certain senior officers and leading members were established. After his retirement early in 1984, again after inviting the chief officers to apply, his successor as Director of Finance was appointed joint Chief Executive/Director of Finance.

Retrenchment: the first administration 1978–82

For the Conservatives, then, the major task was curtailing expenditure. The discussions leading to their first budget in 1979–80 were conducted openly in the Conservative Group in a conference to draw up priorities for cuts. The conference failed to come up with the clearcut recommendations desired by the leadership. Meanwhile the officers, too, were slow in responding to member demands for areas of possible cost reductions. Retrenchment was already proving more difficult than had been expected: 'It was rather like a runaway train, the amount of actual cut as opposed to cut in expectations was quite limited to start with. To stop the thing in its tracks and turn it around is not very easy.'

Consequently in their first year of office the Conservatives only managed savings of 0.5m pounds though in the next year this figure rose to 4.25m pounds. But it was not until early in 1981 that the strains created by retrenchment began to surface in a series of confrontations between the Council and the unions. Over the first two and a half years retrenchment had been relatively easy with the exception of a few controversial decisions, like the Arts Centre, as the slack in the organisation had been taken up. However by the time of the 1981–82 budget the search for cuts led to the first major contest over retrenchment.

The first three years of Conservative rule, then, were relatively peaceful industrially. On the manual side there had just been the continuing problems with the refuse collectors and the street cleansers while on the white collar side there had been only two major local disputes – over re-gradings for typists and for housing management assistants. The white collar disputes at least had been settled amicably on both sides. On the management side the leading members took a very conciliatory approach towards industrial action and did not use sanctions against those taking action, a stance that was to change over the next few years. The officer management, too, were hesitant about the Majority Group's likely response to industrial issues and were cautious in their dealings with the unions, tending to refer most industrial matters to the members for decision. The union side as well were feeling their way after several years of sympathetic Labour administration. But even at this stage the union leadership were very conscious that they were experiencing the calm before the storm:

> all through this time we were very conscious that we were going to be facing compulsory redundancies at some point so this exercised our minds and energies more than anything else . . . everything that we were doing was based on the idea that we had to organise our members for long and serious industrial action over compulsory redundancies. In many ways the comparability dispute and the housing management assistants were dry runs.

The 1981 redundancies dispute

The first major dispute over retrenchment did not arise until early 1981. The Leader, who had assumed the leadership just under a year before, called a press conference on the coming year's budget unilaterally and without informing his political colleagues. The NALGO leadership suspected that a major announcement regarding cuts was about to be made. So they acted quickly and picketed the press conference, only permitting the reporters to enter when the latter had agreed to listen to their point of view afterwards.

At the conference the Leader announced his intention to seek major staff reductions and departmental reorganisations. Overall he targeted staff reductions at 10 per cent or about 700 staff, of whom 400 were to be officer and 300 manual staff. The main departmental change was the absorption of the Planning Department into an enlarged Department of Technical Services.

The NALGO Branch had been anticipating such a move for some time. Already they had built up a strike fund and planned possible industrial action. The Branch officers moved quickly in calling an emergency meeting of the Branch which was addressed by Geoffrey Drain, the then General Secretary of the Union. Conborough was already coming to be seen as a test case of the conflict between the new radical conservatism and the unions.

The meeting voted overwhelming for industrial action and two days later there was a one day strike of all staff, including several chief officers, followed by further selective action. Key workers were pulled out in order to inflict the maximum damage while avoiding any loss of income by the membership. The Union called out the telephonists, the housing cashiers and the fuel supply officers and so was effectively able to halt the work of the Council by bringing out just 50 strategically located workers.

This dispute lasted just under three weeks. Although the striking staff were receiving full pay from the Union, they were becoming uneasy and the Union leadership were doubtful of their ability to keep them out on strike. At the same time the Council leadership was beginning to back away from confrontation and to indicate that they were willing to be more conciliatory and to negotiate. The Personnel Chair began informal discussions with the unions and, in an effort to repair the damage done by the Leader's precipitate announcement, he gave the unions a no compulsory redundancies agreeement conditional on the unions cooperating over reductions in staff numbers and departmental reorganisations. Meanwhile staff numbers would be reduced through the introduction of an attractive voluntary severance scheme.

The staff response to the severance scheme was much greater than anyone had anticipated and it quickly became quite clear that the Conservatives could achieve substantial staff reductions without resort to compulsory redundancies. Despite their concerns with the numbers of jobs being lost, the unions went along with the scheme as large sections of their memberships were obviously intending to vote with their feet by leaving Council employment.

The dispute demonstrated the willingness of the unions,

especially NALGO, to take industrial action to defend the job security of their members. In part the dispute had been caused by the Leader's unilateral action in announcing heavy job cuts in a way that was seen as provocative by the unions. It was the conciliatory approach of the Personnel Chair that had restored the situation by offering the assurance of job security. Notably this offer was not altogether acceptable to all members of the Conservative Group and it drew some flack onto the Chair. However, in the event, it proved to be of considerable importance in easing the shedding of staff. One of the leading members grudgingly accepted that the no compulsory redundancy assurance had proved useful as a means of minimising industrial disruption while still allowing jobs to be shed: 'It was on these fears [for their own jobs] that the unions play so it did have a value in removing at a stroke the fear that they were going to be summarily dismissed. So it was a necessary expedient.'

The first administration and privatisation: the street cleansers

Privatisation was not seriously considered within the Conservative Group until near the end of their first administration. One of the first priorities of the new Conservative Administration had been to sort out the street cleansing and refuse services. These two services had been centres of industrial disruption for some years. The Conservatives had been particularly angered by their experience of the national 1978–79 'Winter of Discontent' action by the manual workers. Moreover the productivity levels of the refuse collection service had been criticised by the District Auditor for several years running but the Council had failed to reach agreement with the unions over a new bonus scheme. Accordingly one of the first actions of the new Administration was to open negotiations with the unions involved, the main one being the GMBATU.

These negotiations dragged on for almost two years. The Council negotiators became very frustrated by what they saw as union intransigence and unwillingness to make concessions as well as by the apparently inconsistent and vacillating approach of the union negotiators. So in July 1980 they adopted a confrontationist approach. They gave the unions an ultimatum that unless the latter agreed to the Council's latest bonus scheme on offer, they would impose it unilaterally on the workforce. The unions protested but finally accepted the scheme under duress. Under the new scheme the refuse workforce was reduced by almost 40 staff.

Meanwhile as far as the Conservatives were concerned the street cleansers were proving even more intransigeant than the refuse collectors. Again the main issues at stake were reductions in numbers and the division of any productivity gains between the employers and the workers. The negotiations were even more prolonged than those with the refuse collectors and by early 1981 there was still no settlement in sight.

In July 1981 the Chair concerned wrote to all the street cleansers expressing his concern with the 'obvious deterioration in the service and the lack of progress over a long period of negotiations aimed at improving matters'. He explained that the Council now felt compelled to ask for outside tenders for the service but that the existing workforce would be able to submit their own tender. However, regardless of the outcome, the Council would honour its no compulsory redundancy agreement.

The unions representing the cleansers retaliated with a circular to all staff which argued that the numbers of cleansers had already been drastically reduced through natural wastage and this, together with poor equipment, had led to the deterioration in the service. A Joint Unions Liaison Committee was formed across the Council's unions and the NALGO Branch voted to support the cleansers through a policy of non-cooperation with outside contractors. The Joint Committee sent a statement round to all the councillors summing up the unions' primary objections to privatisation: 'You must realise that contractors and consultants are anathema to us. Whatever your guarantees now, you cannot guarantee the job security, pay and conditions of our members once they have been hived off to the private sector.'

A few days later there was a one day manual workers strike joined by almost one thousand workers. NALGO did not take strike action but instead tried to initiate a national blacking of all contractors tendering for the street cleansing contract. Essentially they were gambling on the Conservatives' willingness to believe that such a blacking was a real possibility. When the contract was advertised the Union took out advertisements in the same journals stating that any firm tendering might be subject to a national blacking by the trade unions.

The Conservative Council saw this move by NALGO as an act of confrontation and served injunctions on the Branch officials. The Branch Chair went on a quixotic mission to the TUC Conference where he appealed for help to David Basnett, the then General Secretary of the GMBATU, on the grounds that he was faced with legal action while defending Basnett's members. Basnett gave him the brush off. Geoffrey Drain was more sympathetic but could not offer any guarantees that the Union nationally would support the Conborough Branch if the case came to court.

The case never did go to court. Potential contractors had not been deterred by the threat and by early 1982 the tendering process was underway. The unions decided that they had little option but to agree to a council tender being submitted on behalf of the existing workforce and based on a 25% reduction in posts.

In the event the Council turned down the in-house tender and accepted a substantially lower tender from a private contractor. But there were, in line with the Council's earlier assurances, no compulsory redundancies. Most of the existing workforce was offered a job by the contractors although on wages and conditions lower than those in local government; a state of affairs that was to become a major issue in the next dispute over privatisation.

The first administration and privatisation: the refuse collectors

The privatisation of street cleansing in Conborough received considerable publicity. In February 1982 a Minister from the Department of the Environment visited the Borough and commended its approach. During the visit the cleansing contractors presented the Leader with an offer to save the Council up to 5m pounds over the next five years in the refuse service. Officially this was a surprise for the Leader but he later admitted that he had 'not been entirely unaware that this was going to happen'.

Obviously the Council could not accept a tender without going through a competitive process so in March the council advertised for tenders. The Conservatives rejected a proposal from the unions that the Council should wait for staff proposals and a

Labour attempt to commit the Council only to accept as potential contractors those firms who offered pay and conditions comparable to those in local government. Certainly the Conservatives seemed to have recognised that major savings could only really be accomplished by undercutting the service conditions offered in local government.

The unions faced a difficult choice. They could follow the precedent of the street cleansers and negotiate in the hope of lowering costs to make them more competitive with the private sector. Alternatively they could opt for a strategy of confrontation with the employer to deflect them from the path of privatisation. Their concern was that the contractors, simply by offering lower wages and service conditions than those currently enjoyed by their members, would be able to undercut an in-house tender. Additionally there was some concern that the contractors might use the tender as a 'loss leader' to gain a foothold in the potentially enormous local authority refuse collection market. More generally the union leaders did not believe that the Conservatives were seriously interested in giving the tender to their own workforce because they saw the Conservatives' interest in privatisation, particularly that of the Leader, as ideologically motivated. Under these circumstances confrontation was seen as the only winnable, albeit it high risk strategy.

The Trades Union Liason Committee was reconstituted and began preparing a campaign of action to halt privatisation, an aim which the Conservatives from the outset regarded as non-negotiable. For the first time the unions resolved to take their campaign beyond the usual limits of industrial action and into the local community. They began a campaign directed towards the general public and groups of possible supporters through briefing the press, taking press advertisements, distributing leaflets and establishing or renewing contracts with local Labour Party branches, the local Trades Council and local community groups.

Of course the more immediate problem that faced the union leaders was that of managing the discontent of their own memberships. They were certainly very concerned with pressing home to their rank-and-file members what the realities of privatisation would mean for them. In their speeches and publicity they argued that the privatisation of the street cleansers and now the refuse collectors was just the thin end of the wedge that had other council services at the other end. Thus it was in the interests of all employees to oppose the Council's plans. This argument was given added cogency when the local Conservative manifesto was published. The manifesto referred to further possible privatisation initiatives for instance in catering, cleaning, drivers in Social Services and other departments, the running of crematoria and of public conveniences.

White collar professional services were not mentioned specifically in the manifesto, but some Conservative spokesmen had been making it clear that no area of Council activity was necessarily immune. The Conservatives were cautious about their intentions regarding these services, being wary about creating a greater sense of shared interests between NALGO and the manual unions. But the NALGO leadership were anxious to get the message over to their members that privatisation was a real threat to them. In circulars to their members they argued that the Conservative Council was deliberately picking on the services one by one in order 'to stop us mounting a big, unified fight against privatisation in general'. Accordingly 'if refuse goes there will be such demoralisation in the Branch that it will be well nigh impossible to protect the hundreds of white collar jobs that [the Leader of the Council] will turn on next'.

The intention of the Liaison Committee had been to hold a mass meeting of all the Council's trade unionists to initiate a campaign of action. But at the end of March the dustmen voted for strike action and walked off the job. Despite regarding this action as precipitate the Liaison Committee and especially NALGO had little choice other than to support the strikers. However when the meeting did take place, in early April, the Council's unionists voted overwhelmingly in support of the dustmen and of further action.

Despite union hopes that this expression of support would deflect the Conservatives from privatisation, the Leader made it plain that the Council's resolve remained unshaken.

Given the Conservatives' apparent intransigeance the manual unions decided to step up the action. The unions called out all the manual workers, the majority of whom responded to the call. Meanwhile NALGO called a one day strike in mid April and followed it up with selective action similar to that used during the earlier compulsory redundancies dispute. Those NALGO members involved in selective action were the telephonists, the council house sales staff and the fuel supply officers. Other members were instructed not to use the telephones, deal with any outside contractors and perform any extra duties.

This time the response of the employers to this form of action was much tougher than during the earlier dispute. A circular was sent to all staff under the Leader's name. It set out the Council's case, in particular arguing that contracting out could save around 15 per cent from the cost of the refuse service. The circular also stressed that there was still time for the direct labour force to come up with their own proposals for cost cutting. A further circular, this time over the name of the Chief Personnel officer, was sent out to warn staff that all employees who took strike action would not be paid and that those who refused to cross picket lines would be treated the same as the strikers. Staff were told that: 'In the event of industrial action . . . the Council will not be deterred, and will not accept a situation in which refuse is not collected, or in which employees do not do the duties required of them.' Accordingly the Council made arrangements with a contractor to remove the rubbish for the duration of the strike and with an agency to bring in outside telephonists to fill in for the strikers. Finally the unions and staff were given a deadline that unless they resumed normal working by 26 April, they would be suspended without pay.

On the 26th NALGO was still defying the Council. The Conservatives realised that they could find themselves confronted by massive industrial action across all sections of their workforce in the run-up to the local elections. So they backed away from immediate suspensions and extended the deadline. This time those staff persisting with selective action would have their pay docked in proportion to that part of their work they were deemed as not completing.

In the meantime the local elections were now in full swing. The Conservatives decided to use the strike, and perhaps they had little choice by this time, as a major issue and campaigned on the basis of 'Who runs Conborough?' Their case was that as a democratically elected council it was within their rights to decide whether or not to place refuse collection out to tender especially when there was every possibility of real savings to the Council. They were willing to consider any proposals from within the

Council for savings but any direct labour option would have to be tested in competition with other tenders. Thus in press advertisements the Conservatives declared that 'Conborough's Marxist Labour Party is in the pocket of militant trade unionists' and, in an allusion to Alliance candidates, that 'only the Conservatives can keep Conborough out of the red'.

The local Labour Party was uncertain how to respond. Despite pressure from local branches to announce that all privatised services would be returned to direct labour, the Labour Group avoided such a commitment though all Labour candidates did sign a statement declaring support for the dustmen. Much of this uncertainty stemmed from the Labour councillor's concern that the dispute and the strike could cost them the election.

The unions themselves became involved in the election campaign. Trade unionists were active within the local Labour Party. Although their actual numbers within local Labour Party branches were not large, they received considerable sympathy within the branches. The unions also took their case straight to the electorate. They took advertisements in the local press putting their case, particularly stressing the loss of public accountability involved in privatisation. They also produced a four page broadsheet dealing with privatisation and 40 000 were distributed around the Borough. The broadsheet argued the unions' case in dramatic terms:

> The Conborough Conservatives have decided to declare war on their employees on the eve of the Council elections. It is nothing more than a cynical election gimmick. They are trying to make the trade unions the scapegoats for their mismanagement of the Borough's services and the terrible neglect of services.
>
> . . . Our fight is for our members' jobs, our members' living standards and our members' conditions of work. But more than that – we are fighting for the people of Conborough and the services they have a right to expect.

To summarise the situation, then, just prior to the elections: the Conservative ruling group was arguing that their unions were engaged in essentially political and not industrial action as the latter's aim was to overturn decisions made by democratically elected councillors; while the unions were arguing that they were simply protecting their members' legitimate interests in their own jobs, pay and conditions of service.

Refuse privatisation and the council elections

The Conservatives won the 1982 elections but with their majority halved. Like most local elections the results were largely determined by national political rather than by local political factors. Nationally the Falklands War and the rise of the Social Democratic Liberal Alliance were decisive in the Conservatives' electoral revival culminating in their 1983 election victory the following year. However, compared with the neighbouring London boroughs, Conborough had a more pronounced swing away from the Conservatives. This swing suggests that the dispute was, if anything, a slight electoral liability for them.

Immediately after the election the Leader sent out his third notice to all staff:

> The electors of Conborough have made their decision and chosen the policies of the Conservative Party. That is the right place for policies to be put to the test and decided on. Judgements on policies are not for the unions. It is for them to look after the interests of their members within the policies decided on by the electors.

Accordingly the Council would only negotiate with the workforce over the creation of a more cost effective service to be tested against outside tenders. Significantly the Leader replaced the Personnel Chair with the Deputy Leader, reflecting some dissatisfaction with the former Chair's performance and the hope that a new face might increase the chances of a settlement.

Meanwhile cracks had begun appearing in the joint union campaign. A few days after the elections the NALGO Branch voted to stop their action and re-open negotiations. The election results had demoralised NALGO rank and file as well as seriously depleting their strike fund. And it certainly seemed to many NALGO members that they had expended all this effort in fighting someone else's battle.

The manual workers intensified their action. Just four days after the elections the manual workers All London Joint Shop Steward Committee organised a march through the Borough and gathered 10 000 signatories. They also stepped up their picketing of the Council depots and more manual workers joined the refuse collectors on strike.

The new Personnel Chair's approaches to the manual unions, then, were rebuffed. Switching back to a more confrontationist approach, the Council issued an ultimatum. Unless the strikers returned to work within five days, the Council would begin proceedings to sack all strikers on the grounds of breach of contract. However the Council also offered to extend the deadline for the in-house tender and to earmark 800 000 pounds for severance payments to any workers who returned to work but lost their job as a result of privatisation.

At the same time the Council resolved to get tough with the union pickets. Since the start of the strike, the Council's dustcarts had remained in their depots which were heavily picketed. Up to this point the Council had decided not to risk any physical confrontation with the pickets and instead paid the contractors to use their own vehicles. The Conservatives decided that they could no longer tolerate this situation. Early one morning, then, the contractor's men arrived at the depot and removed the carts with the assistance of the police holding the pickets back. Inevitably several pickets were arrested.

After this incident the level of bitterness between the two sides increased considerably. A few days later several of the vehicles removed were mysteriously blown up and some leading Conservative councillors received threatening phone calls against them and their families.

Now that the manual workers strike committee had lost NALGO's support, they tried to get national support from their own unions, NUPE and GMBATU. Votes of support at the two national conferences had only produced minor contributions to the strike fund and ineffectual calls for a national blacking of all street cleansing contractors that were unlikely to be endorsed by the TUC. However the General Secretary of NUPE did write to all Conborough councillors asking them to consider their decision carefully and implying that privatisation could precipitate national action. In Conborough such a threat could only prove counterproductive.

But by this time the strike was crumbling with manual workers from sections other than refuse returning to work. At the end of May the unions gave in and accepted a Council offer to give them sight of the outside tenders and enhanced redundancy payments if necessary.

When the union representatives were given copies of the tenders, they realised immediately that they could not hope to compete. To do so they would have had to agree to a staff cut of over one third.

The Council accepted the lowest tender and gave the existing workers three months notice. Although the contract was awarded on the understanding that the successful firm would give priority to employing existing members of the workforce, the contractor took on less than half of those who applied for their former jobs. So there was some suspicion among the unions that the contractor had discriminated against those shop stewards and others who had been active in the strike.

In the meantime there were further difficulties between the management and NALGO. It will be recalled that they had abandoned their sympathetic action and returned to normal working without any formal understanding with the employer two weeks before the manual workers returned. A few days after their return the Council instructed all chief officers to make deductions of between 20 and 50 per cent from the pay of those involved in the blacking of the telephones during the action. Consequently all the departments had to make a minimum deduction of 20 per cent with the exception of Housing where staff lost 50 per cent of their pay. Despite Union objections the Council refused to negotiate over these deductions which were seen by the Conservatives as a justifiable refusal not to pay for work that was not done.

In conclusion the refuse dispute was the most serious industrial dispute of the two Conservative administrations and created great bitterness on both sides. It was a significant defeat for the unions. From then on privatisation gained momentum in the Borough and the manual workers' unions were never again able to mobilise a major resistance. Similarly the dispute had a seriously demoralising effect on NALGO, as one Branch official ruefully remarked: 'they gave us one hell of a hammering over that one.' There was also some feeling within the Branch that they had been forced by the manual workers to fight on ground not of their own choosing.

From the viewpoint of the Conservative Group the dispute was a success. The Leader was congratulated at the national Conservative Party Conference for facing 'great intimidation and threats' from council workers and having resisted 'anti-democratic and bully boy tactics'. According to press reports of the occasion, the Conborough Leader declared that: 'It has long been accepted for far too long that local authorities are places for mopping up surplus labour. We can't carry on like that any longer.'

The Conservatives, then, had achieved their objective in the face of strong union resistance. Moreover they had pushed home their advantage and breaking with their previously more conciliatory stance had enforced sanctions against the officer staff. These sanctions were intended both as a deterrent and punitive, many Conservative members feeling that officers should not be permitted to get away with taking industrial action while remaining on full pay.

Housing and privatisation

The Conservatives were quick to push their advantage home. The Leader presented his own report to Council recommending that all chief officers should be directed to seek savings by identifying areas of work which could be put out to competitive tender, including areas of manual and white collar work. The report was not subject to the usual twenty-one days notice for staff consultation on the grounds that it was 'a fundamental and integral part of the Majority Party's policies, on which an election has been fought and won, and have therefore been well known to all staff for some considerable time'.

Significantly a few months later the Council formally revoked the earlier no compulsory redundancy agreement. The Conservative leadership argued that new uncertainties, especially created by growing financial constraints and the possible results of introducing competitive tendering, meant that such an agreement was no longer practicable. The Council would give an undertaking to avoid staff redundancies but only as long as staff cooperated with any changes and refrained from restrictive activities such as blackings and refusing to cover for vacant posts. In addition the Council stated that any redeployed staff moved down in grade would only be guaranteed grade protection for one year. There was a strong element of confrontation here, the staff were being *told* what would happen if they did not cooperate.

Over the following months feasibility studies were carried out into the possibility of inviting tenders for architectural, surveying and legal services. These studies, the results of which were not released, indicated that these services could be more cheaply accomplished within the Council. Indeed there were strong arguments for keeping a core of these professional services on tap within the Council to enable the elected members to be advised quickly and reliably and also to monitor the work done by any outside contractors.

The Housing Department now became the focus for privatisation initiatives. In July 1983 the Council asked the company that held the refuse contract to conduct a feasibility study of privatisation on the largest housing estate in the Borough. The estate had been a GLC estate and had been transferred to the Borough in 1979 and, subsequently had had a history of industrial relations difficulties in assimilating the former GLC caretakers into the Borough's conditions of service. Another reason for the interest in privatisation was that it was a self-contained estate easily contracted out to a private estate management company.

As soon as the rumours of a feasibility study reached the union officials, they began to mobilise their members. The three main unions, NALGO, NUPE and GMBATU, had already been meeting together to try to learn from the failure of the refuse strike. They warned their members in a circular that: 'Privatisation can only really work by increasing the exploitation of the workers – that is the only area where a profit margin can succeed.'

NALGO in particular began developing close working relations with local tenants associations. The NALGO leadership took the view that without the support of the users or tenants they would be isolated and defeated. They realised that they had to come up with a serious alternative to privatisation and demonstrate to the tenants that they were really committed to improving the service and not just to their own interests as employees.

Within the Housing Department staff approaches to the Director had not produced any results. The Director refused to negotiate over the feasibility study on the grounds that it was a policy and not an industrial matter, though he gave them the disconcerting assurance that existing staff would be given preferential treatment in their future employment if privatisation took place.

Not surprisingly with the threat of job losses, the Housing staff voted overwhelmingly for non-cooperation with the consultants. The management response was to threaten industrial action against any staff members failing to cooperate with the consultants. The clear message to the staff was that the Council was determined to force this through. The staff were left in no doubt that the Council would not hesitate to apply sanctions against those who took any blacking action as it had during the refuse strike. The Council had used sanctions against staff blacking action during the refuse strike so there could be little doubt that it would do so again.

However the new alliance with the tenants proved its value for the Union. The local tenants association organised a large picket outside the district housing office to prevent the consultants entering. The picket lasted two weeks and forced the consultants to conduct their feasibility study at the Town Hall to which they summoned the district housing officers.

The Council kept up the pressure on NALGO. In early September the Personnel Chair refused to negotiate jointly with the tenants and the Union over the future of the Housing service and circulated a letter to the staff explaining that the feasibility study was a policy decision. Soon after the Department refused to authorise a Union meeting in the Department in breach of the informal understanding that such emergency meetings could be called during disputes. In protest the Housing staff walked out for an hour.

By the end of September the Council leadership changed tack. The consultants had withdrawn unable to complete their work. The Personnel Chair offered to postpone any decisions over the housing service for a further six weeks to allow the unions time to come up with their own proposals.

A month later the NALGO Housing Stewards and the local tenants association produced a joint report. They had formed the impression that the management was sympathetic to such a joint initiative between staff and tenants. Their report was a detailed, eighteen page analysis of the problems in the Department, recognising that low morale was widespread in the Department and that there was a 'substantial measure of disillusionment' among the tenants with the quality of service, points mentioned in an earlier outside report on the department. Notably the housing officers expressed their willingness to work unconventional hours with minimum time in lieu to clear up the backlog of work.

The report also took issue with the Council's expressed intention of moving rent arrears administration into the Finance Department. They argued that this was against professional housing opinion which favoured a comprehensive or integrated housing service and that arrears could be more effectively and humanely dealt with through locally based housing staff in contact with the problems of the tenants rather than dealt with at the Town Hall. Similarly the Report opposed the Council's intention to centralise the repairs service in the Town Hall on similar grounds.

The Housing Chair refused to table the joint report before the Housing Committee. The Union appealed to the Personnel Chair who backed up his colleague in his refusal to negotiate over the principle of Departmental reorganisation with staff and tenants. In any case the inner Conservative leadership had already formed their own proposals which were quite contrary to those of the Union and tenants.

The reorganisation of the housing department

The central housing concerns of the Conservatives were the escalating rent arrears and the poor organisation of the repairs service. Early in 1983 before the present dispute they had called in management consultants, who this time had no direct interest in the privatisation options, to review the repairs service. They had recommended, amongst other things, that the repairs service should be under the control of district housing officers to improve service responsiveness.

Subsequently a Housing Review Team was established, being the Staff Review Team with the Director of Housing. The process of review proved to be very closed. The Review Team refused to negotiate with the staff side and would only accept representations from them. Even within the Housing Department only the Deputy Director, apart from the Director, knew about the deliberations.

This closed consultative process is eloquent of the Conservative members' and also certain chief officers' suspicions of even senior staff.

The Housing reorganisation plans as finally unveiled in December 1983 were a bombshell for NALGO. The number of jobs in the district offices was to be reduced by one half in order to increase the size of the rent arrears section; each officer at district level would now be responsible for 1800 dwellings. Moreover unless enough housing management assistants volunteered for transfer, those regarded as 'surplus' to housing management requirements would be compulsorily transferred to the rent arrears section. The plan accepted that some staff would be demoted but those affected would only be guaranteed grade protection for one year in line with the previous policy statement. Otherwise the consultants' proposal to strengthen the client role of the Director were endorsed but, instead of strengthening the control of district officers over repairs, the plans included the centralisation of repairs in the Town Hall. There were a few other minor staff changes as well, most notably the post occupied by the NALGO Secretary was to be deleted. The annual savings arising from the whole plan were estimated as about £90 000.

Negotiations between the two sides opened just before Christmas 1983. The staff side felt very vulnerable as a major departmental reorganisation was about to take place in the absence of any no compulsory redundancy guarantees or redeployment agreements. The Council side refused to give any guarantees over redundancies and to give ground on the grading issue. The staff side felt that the Council was not so much negotiating as stalling.

NALGO once again set its campaign machine into action. All councillors received a fact sheet comparing the latest plans with the earlier management consultant's report and the joint union-tenant report. Local tenants' associations were circulated with details of the proposed changes and warned of the likely consequences for the service, in the Union's view, should the plans be implemented – declining levels of service, a more punitive approach to rent arrears and the possible privatisation of parts of the housing service.

In mid January 1984 NALGO called a meeting of all Housing staff. Prior to the Union meeting, the Director addressed the staff and distributed a broadsheet giving the management's point of view. He did this against his own inclination but was strongly advised to do so by the Personnel Department. However the Union meeting passed a motion, with only four votes against, threatening complete non-cooperation with the reorganisation and indefinite strike action if the employers went ahead with the proposals. The meeting also called on the Council to consider the Union-tenant report, to agree a no compulsory redundancy guarantee and to protect existing grades. Five days later, at an emergency meeting of the whole Branch, it was agreed to build up a strike fund of five pounds a week per member. The Branch Secretary was quoted in the local press as saying, with more bravado than realism: 'People have recognised that this is the crunch and we know that the Union is capable of financing a long dispute' and 'if they try to force this through regardlesss, we'll be straight out'.

Not to be outdone the Leader responded with his own rhetoric. In the local press he claimed that the Union was being 'precipitate' by attempting 'to intimidate us while we are still negotiating.' At this stage he appears to have thought that he could call the Union's bluff: 'If they want us to firm up our position, this kind of black-mail attempt is the way to make us do it. I don't think they will go on strike in any case. At least half the officers in the Housing Department support what we're trying to do.'

Despite these words the Conservative leadership had been surprised by the degree of opposition in the Housing Department. A few days after these rhetorical exchanges, the Council gave ground on the gradings issue and agreed to protect existing grades for the life of their Administration. In fact the Council's original stance on gradings appears to have been a negotiating ploy, holding back a possible (and not very costly) concession as a bargaining chip. As one senior management officer observed drily: 'I can't honestly think that [the Personnel Chair] ever thought that he was going to get away with that . . . they certainly with-drew very fast and they did not wait for any action to take place. They conceded almost immediately so I think he was just playing games.'

The Council side also agreed to a Union demand that the selection procedures for the new posts should be agreed at joint inter-departmental consultative committees of the Finance, Housing and Architects Departments. The Union fear was that certain staff in Housing would be victimised by being selected for down-grading during the reorganisation. On the other issues at stake the Union leadership had to give way. The Council had made it plain that only the details and not the principles of the reorganisation were negotiable and they had already convincingly demonstrated their determination not to shift on such issues of principle during the refuse dispute almost a year earlier.

The building society dispute

Hardly had this dispute been resolved than another dispute flared up in the Department. The Council leadership without consultation signed an agreement with a building society for one district housing office to act as agents for the society for a trial period. NALGO reacted angrily when they heard of the agreement. The Union and staff side view was that it was another attempt by the Council to introduce privatisation. A Union representative also told the local press that 'the public servants' reputation for impartiality is in jeopardy if there is to be a requirement placed on any officer to promote the interests of a particular commercial organisation' and that public resources were about to be used for private gain. The basis for this argument was that the housing cashiers would, in the Council's own words, 'soft sell' the society. The Union representative went on to say:

> This is privatisation by stealth. The Council is having another go at privatising in a piecemeal fashion. They are also attempting to change fundamentally working practices without even consulting staff representatives. It is typical of this Council's secretive, heavy handed approach. We have already seen this approach in their avowed commitment to sell off council housing.

Once again NALGO and the local tenants' association began a joint campaign. The association distributed a leaflet opposing the Council's plan. The leaflet claimed that the plan was a prelude to the forced sale of houses and implied that the society would be given access to tenants' housing records. The Leader of the

Council condemned the leaflet in the local press as 'scurrilous and irresponsible'.

NALGO and the tenants also began picketing the local branch of the building society. The NALGO Secretary phoned the local manager of the society who expressed his fear that he was becoming a 'political football' caught between the Council and the Union. He also admitted that the Leader had been placing pressure on him to stick with the agreement regardless, even assuring him that the Council would guarantee the agreement through using non-union labour if NALGO took industrial action. The prospect of becoming embroiled in an industrial dispute for such a small amount of business was a daunting one. In mid April the society politely withdrew from the agreement until 'the Council clears its lines of communication with tenants and workers'.

The Leader expressed his regret in the local press that an 'imaginative initiative' that 'would have kept the rents and rates down by making money from selling a Council service to the private sector' had been lost. He described the union's and tenants association's fears of privatisation as 'pure paranoia'. Nevertheless from their view the initial secrecy, the avoidance of the agreed consultative channels and the apparent urgency could be seen as providing some basis for that paranoia.

5 Radical Labourism and the Unions

Introduction

There was a long history of Labour rule in Labton. The Party had controlled the Council since its creation in 1963 except for a period of Conservative rule between 1968 and 1971. Labton typified many of the recent political changes within the Labour Party mentioned in Chapter 2. The new ideological politcs appeared on the Council after the 1978 elections when a number of more radical councillors joined the Council and by the time of the 1982 elections the Labour Group had acquired a substantial baggage of policy commitments. These commitments included policies on the decentralisation of council services, economic development initiatives in the Borough, the ethnic monitoring of Council staff and the establishment of a women's committee and support unit.

There are two main themes in this chapter. The first is the growing tension between the Conservative central government intent on reducing expenditure and Labton as a radical Labour council. The second is that of the difficulties experienced by the Labton councillors in reconciling high policy expectations with a reduced availability of resources.

The political leadership 1978–85

Politically Labton was more volatile than Conborough. Between 1978 and 1985, the years covered in this chapter, there were four changes in Council Leader. These changes reflected shifting factional alliances within the Group, whereas the leadership changes in Conborough arose from changed personal circumstances rather than factional competition. This political volatility and factionalism in Labton made the task of leadership difficult and precarious. The problems attached to the task are reflected

93

in the high turnover of leaders. The first Leader during the study period resigned in 1980 for personal reasons. His successor lasted for two years until after the May 1982 local elections when she lost the job following the enlargement of the electoral college that elected the leader to include not only the Labour Group but also representatives of the District Labour Party. This change of leader represented a significant break in terms of the style of group leadership. Whereas the two previous Leaders had tried to lead on a consensual basis, the third Leader was more abrasive and tried to lead more actively. Most notably he began to strengthen the position of leader by developing a Leader's Office with its own staff so providing himself with an important resource *vis-à-vis* the rest of the Group and the officer structure. The fourth Leader, elected after the collapse of the Council's opposition to rate-capping in May 1985, continued with this process of building up the position of leader.

Industrial relations within Labton had historically been fairly harmonious. However once the financial screws tightened on the Council, new tensions began to emerge in the management-union relationship. The management problems of coping with these tensions were compounded by the ideological and organisational affinities between the Labour councillors and the unions, as will be seen in the course of this chapter. These affinities were associated with a management strategy of collaboration with the unions and a comparatively generous management approach to conditions of service matters.

The management response to the growing industrial tensions was to reorganise and strengthen the personnel function within the authority. Until 1982 the personnel function had had only junior status and reported directly to the Chief Executive. The neglect of this function had been worsened by the absence of the then principal personnel officer through illness. After the departure of this officer early in 1982, the Labour Leadership resolved to improve the function and to raise its status within the Authority. This decision was influenced not just by the state of industrial relations but also by the introduction of new equal opportunity policies requiring an enlarged personnel function. Consequently the personnel Department was reorganised and reconstituted towards the end of 1982 and soon after a new Chief Personnel

Officer (CPO) was appointed, interestingly from the private sector, and the Department given full departmental status.

In the following year, a new system of personnel services advisers was introduced. These personnel services advisers (PSAs) were appointed at senior level and given the right of direct access to the Personnel Chair without reference to the CPO, a right that was often used. The PSAs almost routinely phoned the Chair at home and, in turn, were directly contacted by the Chair with whom they were on first name terms. The four PSAs each had responsibility for two or three departments and were members of the departmental management teams, in fact they were senior to the departmental personnel officers. The aim of the PSA system was to correct the centrifugal effects of departmentalism by tightening up central control over personnel and industrial relations in the departments. The PSAs were put in place to ensure greater consistency of policy across departments and to enable the management side to respond more rapidly and more sensitively to emerging industrial problems and disputes. Their appointments were made at a senior level both to enhance their authority and to interest able people, notably two of the PSAs were former staff side secretaries in Labton.

The low pay issue

Between 1978 and 1982 the main points of industrial unrest were the refuse collection service and the Town Hall porters. The low level of productivity in the refuse service, compared with other authorities, had concerned Council members and officers for some years. Despite these concerns the management side had been unable to reach agreement with unions on a revised productivity scheme. The Labour leadership increased the pressure on the unions to renegotiate the refuse productivity scheme during 1981 but agreement was only finally reached just before the May 1982 elections. The minds of the unionists had been concentrated by the possibility that the Conservatives might gain control of the Borough and prove tougher negotiators than Labour and possibly even privatise the service. The unionists, then, saw a settlement prior to the election as expedient and so agreed to a new productivity scheme involving annual savings to the Council of about 400 000 pounds.

The next industrial difficulty arose several weeks after the 1982 local elections when the Town Hall porters took strike action. It was the first serious industrial action in Labton since the national 'Dirty Jobs' strike of 1978–79. The strike was primarily over the differentials between those manual workers, like the porters, who had little or no opportunity to earn bonus payments through productivity gains and those workers, like the dustmen, who did receive such bonuses. The porters were understandably anxious to close the pay differential between them and the dustmen so, at least indirectly, the strike arose from the refuse workers settlement.

This concern over manual worker differentials had a history in Labton. The question of differentials had been raised several times over recent years, according to the two unions involved (TGWU and NUPE), but no action had been taken by the Council. The new Labour Administration, elected in 1982, had pledged to do something about low pay among council workers in their manifesto. So the unions believed that the time was right to press their members' case through immediate action.

The initial reaction of the Labour councillors was a mixture of political embarrassment and sympathy for the porters' case. Suddenly they were undergoing the experience of being portrayed as hard faced employers within and outside the Council. There was a surge of sympathy for the porters from among local Labour Party branches, encouraged by the activities of unions who leafletted and spoke to local party branches. So from the very first the dispute was waged in the wider political arena as well as within 'normal' industrial relations channels.

As the employers the Labour leadership had to cope with two main problems. The first was the narrow industrial relations problem that to give in to the porters' demands would quite likely set off a series of further comparability claims from similarly placed blue collar workers such as caretakers, social services drivers and assistants. At a time of financial restraint the effect of such leapfrogging claims would have been very serious and have raised further doubts about the financial feasibility of new policy intitiatives.

The second problem was the wider one of political management.

The political leaders had both to cope with the pressures, sympathetic to the unions, emanating from the Party and to maintain their authority within the Group to ensure their political future yet hold a consistent managment line at the same time. During the porters' dispute the Chair of Personnel tried to contain negotiations with the unions to the formal channels in the face of pressures favouring the use of informal channels. These pressures were difficult to contain as members of the Labour Group leaked details of the management negotiating stance to union officials. A rival Chair at one point even opened up his own point of negotiation with the unions and had to be censured by his colleagues, significantly he lost his Chair in the next group elections.

The porters' strike was resolved after two weeks. The union officials settled for less than their original claim, agreeing to the Council's final offer to double their flat rate bonus plus a small regrading increase and improved pension arrangements. The Council made the agreement on the basis that the manual unions would not use it as a lever in pressing for yet more comparability claims, Instead the Council, in line with their manifesto promise, agreed to an investigation of low pay among the workforce and further action to combat low pay. As a result the Council and unions agreed to a new Low Pay Initiative early in 1983. Under this Initiative the Council agreed to provide over half a million pounds to raise the incomes of those employees paid beneath the official poverty line.

The turning point

During 1983 relationships between the Council and the unions, especially NALGO, deteriorated significantly. The Labour Group was experiencing growing problems in accommodating new policy initiatives within increased financial constraints. Financial constraint not only limited such initiatives but also reduced the ability of management to gain the co-operation of staff through regrading and career incentives. Yet the widely held expectation in the Labour Group was that the unions would and should collaborate with the Group in carrying out policies obviously in the interests of the Labour Movement. This expectation was reinforced by the view that the Council had made major service conditions concessions to the unions over recent years so the councillors could point, for example, to the Low Pay Initiative and a generous maternity/paternity scheme introduced in 1982.

Meanwhile the unions, especially NALGO whose members were most affected by policy changes, resisted cooptation by the employer. During 1983 it became clear that the unions were unwilling to compromise what they saw as legitimate pay and conditions demands to facilitate the introduction of new policies even though many of the union leaders personally sympathised with Labour's aims.

In any case union officials harboured doubts about the willingness of the Labour Group to maintain real spending levels. By this time central government pressure on local spending had become very intense with the introduction of targets and penalties and the threat of rate-capping on the horizon (see Chapter 2). Consequently many local union leaders concluded that they had to apply continuing pressure on the Labour councillors to deter them from giving in to government pressures. If the unions allowed themselves to be coopted, the concern was that the position of those in the Labour Group who favoured some trimming of expenditure would be strengthened. This distrust of the intentions of the Labour leadership increased as the latter tightened their control over the running of the authority and, for instance, began to vet all vacancies centrally before advertising posts.

The growing distrust and uncertainty over employer intentions led the unions to seek ways of limiting management discretion to deploy staff. The leaders of the main unions pressed the Council to avoid the use of temporary and agency staff where permanent staff could be employed. NALGO, in particular, was concerned that the Council was making covert savings by manipulating the vacancy factor and leaving jobs vacant for an unreasonable length of time. Such manipulation was seen as the thin end of a wedge which had job cuts at the other end as well as increasing the workloads of existing staff. A related issue, raised just by NALGO, was over job descriptions which the Union wanted to see more tightly defined to limit management discretion. But more importantly NALGO tried to control management's ability to redeploy staff within the authority through boycotting jobs in the new Economic Development Unit and the Women's Support

Unit. These actions formed a particular source of annoyance within the Labour Group.

Nevertheless the Labour leadership remained anxious to maintain good relationships with the unions. Early in 1983 the management side offered significant concessions to the unions. Although the management side emphasised in the JCC meetings that they had only used temporary and agency staff when really necessary, they offered the unions a formal understanding not to appoint such staff unless there were special circumstances such as staff sickness or special leave. As part of the understanding they agreed to provide the employee sides with details of all vacancies and the arrangements made to fill them, and also agreed to improve consultation over changes in office accommodation. However the employer side refused NALGO's demand for more tightly defined job descriptions because they regarded such a demand as placing a quite unreasonable restriction on management's ability to manage.

Decentralisation: a major policy initiative

The major organisational change proposed in the 1982 Labton Labour manifesto was the decentralisation of council services into neighbourhood or local offices. Moves towards decentralisation had already begun in the Housing Department some two years earlier, initiated by a second tier officer. Initially two pilot housing neighbourhood offices were set up in 1980 for a two year experimental period. By the time of the 1982 local elections decentralisation had become fashionable in national Labour circles and was included in the Labton Manifesto. After the elections two working groups were set up to consider proposals for council-wide decentralisation of services. One working group was at member level and initially included representatives of the District Labour Party, these representatives were later dropped when the Group thought that the proposals had reached the stage at which only the elected councillors should take the decisions. The other working party was at officer level and took responsibility for the more detailed planning and costing of the proposals.

It was not until September 1983 that the working groups came up with preliminary proposals and it took a further six months for the Council to finalise them. Originally thirteen neighbourhood offices had been visualised but these proposals reduced that number to just four offices covering five wards in the Labour part of the Borough. The proposals were also watered down in terms of service functions, being essentially an extension of the earlier housing decentralisation with the addition of environmental health and community work.

Until this point neither the staff side nor the unions had been brought into any formal consultations over decentralisation. The Labour group had seen the formulation of proposals as essentially a policy matter and therefore as non-negotiable. Similarly during the earlier housing decentralisation, consultation and negotiation had been left until implementation when matters such as regradings for those moved to new posts and changes in working conditions had been negotiated. During these negotiations NALGO had submitted a claim for an annual 300 pound 'dislocation allowance' payable to those officers obliged to move to new offices. This claim had been left on the table. The Labour Group saw the claim as quite impossible to meet since it would render the cost of decentralisation prohibitive. As one senior officer observed: 'You can either see this [decentralisation] as a threat or a challenge and the trade union leadership has accepted it as a challenge but at the same time they are trying to milk as much as they can out of it.'

During the second decentralisation initiative formal union consultations were again left to the implementation stage. There had been a proposal from the officer level working party that the staff side should be involved in the initial planning stages of decentralisation but the Labour Group had rejected the proposal. The view of the Group members had been that such consultations would be premature as they were awaiting the recommendations of the working parties before agreeing a course of action. In addition there was the underlying 'feeling of antipathy', in the words of one senior officer, towards NALGO within the Labour group that had developed after what was seen as uncooperative behaviour by NALGO.

More generally elected member interest in decentralisation had begun to flag. There were serious doubts about the wisdom of committing the Council to such an expensive policy initiative in such an adverse financial climate. Many Labour councillors, too, were realising that the proposed neighbourhood committees could pose a political threat to their position especially in Conservative parts of the Borough where to create such committees would be to give the Conservatives a political platform.

Perhaps surprisingly NALGO did not press for early consultations with management. The Union adopted a 'wait and see' attitude, an attitude that reflected both a scepticism about management commitment to decentralisation and a limited conception of the scope of bargaining. Firstly NALGO kept in close contact with opinion shifts within the Labour Group through various informal channels (One NALGO activist was Chair of the District Labour Party during 1983 for example). Such contact led the Union leaders to doubt the continuing commitment of the Labour Group to decentralisation as the expenditure implications became clearer. Moreover some Union leaders began to think that decentralisation was unjustifiable once central government financial pressures became a serious threat to jobs in Labton. The net effect of these considerations was to incline the Union away from pressing for early consultations – such consultations seemed likely to prove pointless if the policy was dropped and also contained the danger that differences of view over decentralisation among the Union leaders themselves would undermine any attempts by the Union to negotiate.

Secondly the NALGO leaders preferred to limit the scope of bargaining over decentralisation, and indeed over many other issues, to questions of service conditions. In part this preference arose from a concern that any negotiations over policy questions would weaken the political stability of the union, the task of union leadership being further complicated by any policy differences over matters like decentralisation. The Union leaders were also concerned to maintain their position by anticipating likely rank and file demands for compensation payments for any personal disruption, especially where decentralisation seemed likely to increase their journeys to work.

Strike in direct works

The future of the Labton Direct Works Department had become a major concern for both the Labour Group and the unions by early 1982. The workload of the Department was falling off as heavy central government cuts in local authority capital spending began to bite. In addition the requirements of the Land and Planning Act 1980 demanded changes in the orgnaisation of the Department as well as raising doubts about its viability. This Act required local authorities to re-establish their direct labour organisations as separate, commercially viable organisations which had to compete for council work (above certain levels) on the same basis as private contractors. The pre-1982 Labour leadership had recognised the need to reorganise the Department but had failed to reach an agreement with the unions.

Negotiations over organisational change were complicated by the serious tensions within the Department – particularly those between the senior Departmental managers and the craft workers and between the junior white collar supervisors and craft workers whom they supervised. Allegations of inefficiency and incompetency were exchanged between white and blue collar staff, each of whom held the other primarily responsible for the state of the Department. By the Autumn of 1982 relationships had deteriorated badly and management and workers seemed locked into a spiral of distrust.

The new Labour leadership determined to sort out the Department after the May 1982 local elections. After informal negotiations with the craft unions, a joint Council–union Steering Group was set up in November 1982 comprised of councillors, senior Department managers and union representatives. The aim of the Steering Group was stated as the improvement of the Department and, more specifically, raising the quality of management. In the interim the Group itself was to take over the running of the Department. Significantly the staff side in the Department at first refused the invitation to join the Group. Their refusal arose from a suspicion that the Steering Group was a tie-up between the Labour councillors and the craft unions, a suspicion fuelled by the fact that the original invitation to join the Group had been conveyed through one of the craft convenors. Moreover there was a feeling among the Department managers that the councillors were usurping their role and casting doubts over their competence by taking over direct control.

A major part of the Steering Group's work was the reorganisation of the Housing Rehabilitation Group (HRG) section of Direct Works on cooperative lines. This 'partnership experiment', implemented in early 1983, divided the HRG into small teams of about twenty. Each team was headed by a supervisor, surveyor and designer but all members of the team were to be involved in developing the team's work programme, in revising progress and in contributing to decision making within their team. Notably the bonus payments or 'profits' of each team were to be paid on a team not an individual basis. thus the skills of the supervisor and surveyor in maintaining the flow of work and deploying the craftsmen were critical in determining bonus levels, yet the former were paid on a salaried not a bonus basis.

The new posts in the reorganised section were advertised early in 1983. A mixture of existing staff, including some craftsmen, and new staff mostly from the private sector were appointed to head up the teams. One of the newly appointed supervisors was Fred Jones. Jones was appointed in April 1983 and the following August he was summoned to what he assumed was a routine review of his progress as a new probationary employee. At the review the senior managers present expressed concern with his performance, in particular over what they saw as his excessive car mileage claims and his failure to hand over two jobs by the completion date. The managers were dissatisfied with Jones' explanations and indicated that they intended to instigate procedures for Jones' dismissal before his probationary six months were up. They fixed the dismissal hearing for a few days later (to allow them to give him a month's notice of dismissal as a probationer).

Apparently stunned and surprised by this action, Jones and his shop steward went straight to the NALGO Branch Secretary. On the latter's advice Jones requested a postponement of the disciplinary hearing. The Direct Works managers rejected the request which they saw as a delaying tactic as they were anxious to dismiss him within the probationary period thereby avoiding the complications that would arise once he became a permanent employee (such as the right of appeal to a panel of elected members).

The Department managers went ahead with the dismissal hearing in Jones' absence. As soon as the NALGO Secretary heard what was happening, he phoned the Chief Personnel Officer and threatened immediate industrial action unless the hearing was postponed within the hour. The CPO himself had only just heard about the hearing from the Direct Works management. He phoned the Department and thought he had obtained their agreement to think again. He also sent a personnel services adviser across to Direct Works. The adviser was told to persuade the Department managers to settle for a warning and give Jones a second chance by extending the probationary period. But by the time the adviser arrived at the Department, it was too late – the local managers had gone ahead and confirmed the dismissal.

Meanwhile news of Jones' dismissal spread through the Department during the afternoon. The NALGO Secretary arrived and addressed a meeting of his members, arguing that justice had not been done as Jones' right of appeal as a probationer to the CPO had been denied him by the Department management. The meeting voted to walk off the job for the rest of the afternoon.

That was the Friday. On the following Monday a second meeting of the Direct Works NALGO membership was held and supported the Branch Secretary's recommendation that they should demand the intervention of the Personnel Chair as the CPO had not used his power to veto the dismissal. The Secretary wrote to the Chair demanding that he intervene and rescind the dismissal notice by ten o'clock the following morning.

Later the same day the CPO and the Direct Works Manager met with the Branch Secretary. Prior to the meeting the CPO tried to persuade the Department management to agree to lift the dismissal pending an inquiry by him as CPO, a right of appeal contained within the Council's Code of Practice for Probationary Appointments. The Direct Works bosses were unmoved. They had already contacted their Chair who had given them to understand that he supported their stance. At the meeting with the NALGO Secretary, then, the CPO felt that he had no choice but to line up with the Direct Works Management. The meeting was bad tempered and relations became more polarised. The NALGO Secretary now rejected out of hand the suggestion that the CPO should arbitrate on the matter, arguing that the CPO had by then ceased to be an independent arbitrator.

After the meeting the NALGO Secretary, feeling that he had got nowhere with the officer management, phoned the Personnel Chair at home and urged him to intervene. Having already been angered by the letter giving him less than twenty-four hours to act, the Chair was less than sympathetic. He expressed the view that only the officer managers, not the elected members should deal with probationary officers, as probationers had no right of appeal to the members. In his view as Chair the matter should and could easily be sorted out before the expiry of Jones' dismissal notice. These views were conveyed to the Union in a letter he sent to NALGO the next day.

The action spreads

NALGO called a meeting in Direct Works for ten o'clock the next morning. Much to the annoyance of the Union leadership, the Manager of Direct Works called his own meeting for nine o'clock that morning to explain the management point of view. Despite an attempt by the Union to picket the meeting, most staff went along. The NALGO staff meeting immediately afterwards rejected a motion for immediate strike action. However before the meeting could consider other forms of action, it had to be adjourned until the afternoon because a dance class was scheduled to use the hall from eleven o'clock. The meeting reconvened in the afternoon and the strike motion was again put to the meeting and this time was passed. The strike motion declared that the Direct Works staff would strike until the dismissal notice against Jones was suspended pending a full investigation and until assurances were given by management that they would in future respect agreed disciplinary procedures. The afternoon meeting was dominated by staff from Jones' own section, the Housing Rehabilitation Group, who supported action while many other staff from the Department raised doubts about the wisdom of immediate action.

Nevertheless most NALGO members in the Daprtment were on strike by the next day and Council depots were picketed. On the same day the action was given official recognition by NALGO nationally and accordingly all strikers were guaranteed 60 per cent strike pay. The news of the strike and its official recognition was circulated to all NALGO members in the first of a series of broadsheets that were sent out daily throughout the dispute. Shop stewards were also kept informed throughout the dispute from then onwards through daily meetings. By the end of the Tuesday almost 800 NALGO members were out on strike.

By this time alarm had spread within the Labour Group over

the rapid escalation of the action. The Group leadership met on the Wednesday and concluded that they had to back up the officer management despite the latter's technical breaking of agreed procedures.

Of course the Labour Group's resolve to remain firm was strengthened by their view that NALGO had been increasingly unhelpful and even intransigent. At the meeting the Group leadership formed a small officer-member coordinating group to oversee the management side of the dispute. They also decided to appeal directly to the rank and file membership of NALGO by sending a letter over the Leader's name to explain the management position and counter the NALGO broadsheets.

By the Friday, a week into the dispute, over half the white collar staff were out on strike. The strike had snowballed as one department after another had met and voted to join the action. The NALGO leadership by this time was portraying the dispute as being over job security – 'Fred Jones is Down the Road – Are You Next?' – and claiming, by implication, that the Council had deliberately broken agreements with the Union – 'We must not allow the Council to tear up its agreements with us, or to arbitrarily set parts of them aside' (both quotes taken from NALGO strike bulletins).

On the Thursday there had been a meeting of Union representatives and officer management. The officers repeated the earlier offer of arbitration by the CPO and this time stressed that Jones' dismissal would be suspended pending its result. The Union rejected this offer on the grounds that the CPO had lined up with the Direct Works management and so was no longer a 'neutral' arbitrator. While the two sides may well have reached agreement on this basis six days before, events had now made agreement on these lines much more difficult.

On the Friday the member-officer coordinating group met with the NALGO representatives. NALGO modified their position and asked that Jones be reinstated for a further probationary period and his progress be reviewed in line with the Code of Practice for Probationers. The management too modified their position and offered independent arbitration by a panel of elected members with Jones' reinstatement conditional on the outcome. The management offer was put to a shop stewards' meeting to recommend its rejection by the membership. On the Monday a mass meeting of the Branch supported this recommendation by a three to one majority.

In the meantime the Leader's letter had been distributed to all staff. The letter explained the Council's view that the Code of Practice had been followed and that Jones himself had failed to appeal to the CPO. Implicitly countering the NALGO propaganda, the Leader protested that 'there is no evidence to suggest that the Council dismisses any employees without good reason and after careful consideration'.

The Union leadership retaliated with their own letter. They claimed that the Council had embarked on a 'campaign of lies and misinformation' in the 'most disgraceful attempt yet to confuse people and cover up for the mistakes made by management which caused the dispute'. They implied that the Leader was acting as the mouthpiece of senior officer management by adding that the 'whisperings and rumours already spreading have now been followed by this letter distributed by your Senior Managers'. In particular the Union was incensed that the Leader's letter had given the impression that the Code of Practice had been followed when, by this time, the officer management had privately admitted that the Direct Works management had broken the Code.

On the Monday the leader sent out a second letter to staff setting out the offer of elected member arbitration. At a further meeting that day with the member-officer coordinating group, the Union rejected the proposal on the grounds that the elected members themselves were now so identified with the officer management line that their status as independent arbitrators had been too compromised. Instead as a last resort it was agreed to call in the government Arbitration and Conciliation Advisory Service (ACAS) and the ACAS mediators arrived the following day.

The full Labour Group had not met since the start of the dispute. On the Tuesday an emergency meeting of the Group was called to consider the strike. The meeting produced a considerable display of unity within the Group and they passed a resolution supporting the actions of their Group leadership with only two dissenting votes. The main disagreement within the Group was between those who wanted to tough it out further with NALGO and those who favoured an early compromise. The compromisers swayed the Group which resolved to withdraw Jones' dismissal and to suspend him on full pay (not to reinstate him) pending the outcome of an inquiry by a group of elected members.

By this time growing pressure from the blue collar workers was being felt within the Party Group. Some Finance Department staff, the last department to join the action, had walked out on the Tuesday and their action was threatening to disrupt the payment of the weekly paid blue collar workers. The blue collar unions warned the Labour group and NALGO that unless their members were paid 'all hell would break out'. Moreover the NALGO leaders themselves were beginning to lose their nerve in the face of the rapid escalation of the dispute and the unexpected instransigence of the Party group.

Under these pressures the two sides, aided by the ACAS concili-ators, agreed to ask the Joint Secretaries of the Greater London Whitley Council to conduct an inquiry. Both sides agreed to be bound by the results of the inquiry. In the meantime, Jones was to be suspended on full pay. On the return to work both sides also agreed that there would be no victimisation or retaliation by either side and that the Code of Practice on probationers should be revised. Accordingly, after a strike of almost two weeks duration which had come to involve a majority of the white collar workforce, the strikers returned to work.

The dispute peters out

The GLWC Joint Secretaries reported in January 1984. In their Report they identified the root problem as being in the deterior-ating relationships within the Direct Works Department and the immediate causes of the dispute as laying in poor judgements made by key actors in the course of the dispute. They noted that Departmental managers had come to see NALGO as suspicious and obstructive and unwilling to recognise the need for change in the Department. Moreover the elected members tended to compare the attitudes of NALGO unfavourably with what they saw as the more helpful attitudes among the craft unions. Mean-while, on the Union side, the Joint Secretaries thought that the NALGO leadership had become too distrustful of Departmental management. The Union leadership had seen the Jones case not as an aberration but as a precedent because they believed that the management were adopting a new tough managerial approach. This polarisation of attitudes led to the dispute becoming, in the Joint Secretaries' words, a 'test of strength and credibility; almost always fatal to a speedy resolution of the issues'.

In terms of the more immediate causes of the dispute, the Joint Secretaries raised questions over the actions of the various actors in the development of the dispute. In their view the Labton Joint Secretaries should have intervened earlier, on the first Monday, to lift Jones' dismissal pending an inquiry by the CPO. Instead the Personnel Department had succumbed to pressure from the Direct Works management to back them up – the latter fearing that to revoke the dismissal would weaken their management credibility. Moreover the GLWC Joint Secretaries argued that if it had been explained on the Monday to the NALGO Secretary that the CPO's inquiry would have been linked to the temporary suspension rather than the dismissal of Jones, the Union leadership might have stopped the action. Even so the NALGO Secretary himself should have been aware of this possibility and both he and his colleagues should have been less inclined to adopt an intransigent attitude towards the employers

The Joint Secretaries also commented on the respective roles of the elected and appointed management. In principle, they argued, elected members should not become involved in a dispute at too early a stage. Elected members should only be involved when 'all avenues should first have been explored and seen to have failed, if for want of no better practical reason, that elected members are then able to provide an independent and further level of recourse'. In particular the Report questioned the wisdom of the Leader sending two letters to the staff as the content of these letters contributed to the later allegation of lack of independence on the part of the elected members which led, in particular, to Union resistance to the idea of a member level inquiry into the case. Instead it recommended that such letters should be sent out in the name of the Chief Executive.

The Joint Secretaries' Report was inconclusive. It allocated blame and repsonsibility evenly to both sides and avoided any judgements on the allegations against Jones. The Council appointed a panel of three elected members to draw up the employer response. Notably the three panel members selected were members who had been relatively distant from the dispute, the Chair of the Panel, for example, having been on holiday during the dispute. In its Report the Panel accepted the Joint Secretaries' criticisms relating to the management of Direct Works and the Steering Group. They recommended improvements to the training of both managers and unionists in jointly agreed procedures relating to matters like discipline. However on the particular issue of Jones' employment, they concluded that he was 'guilty of misconduct and that his employment should be discontinued forthwith'.

NALGO responded angrily to the Panel Report. The Union Secretary condemned the Report at the January Branch Executive and circulated a letter to all Union members which criticised it as a 'whitewash' of the management's actions and claimed that there was a 'a fast moving line for the chop' from the Council's payroll. The NALGO Executive reommended that the Panel Report be rejected and a Branch meeting confirmed the recommendation with 550 for, 300 against and 44 abstentions. The Branch renewed the demand that Jones be reinstated and threatened industrial action in the form of a one day strike at the end of February, a campaign of lightening half day strikes, a boycott of sources of Council income and a regular lobby of Council meetings.

The Labour Group ignored the demand for Jones' reinstatement. In their view they had acted in accordance with the original agreement to stand by the Joint Secretaries' Report. Informally they also took the view that NALGO had shot its bolt and that now, more than four months after the strike, it is unlikely that the union could marshall its members and carry out these threats.

The Union was able to get several hundred staff out on the one day strike. But it quickly became clear that the leadership lacked the rank-and-file support to sustain a campaign of industrial action. In addition the call to disrupt Council revenues was pointless given the low level of militancy in the finance Department, the last Department to take action during the dispute. The impetus for continued action was further diminished when the Branch Secretary resigned after allegations of financial mismanagement. The new Secretary lacked his predecessor's commitment to the issue and together with other Branch leaders was anxious to get the Jones case off the Union agenda. The issue smouldered on, Jones insisted that he still wished to be reinstated, although he had found other work, and the hard left faction on the Branch Executive continued to press his case. The Council made several attempts to arrange a severance settlement with Jones but without success. The issue has never been formally resolved.

The rate-capping crisis

Central government had been tightening the financial screws on local government since the mid seventies. In Labton the central government block grant fell from 54 per cent to 39 per cent of total Council revenues between 1978–79 and 1984–85. Over this period Labton had actually slightly increased spending in real terms and had made up for the loss of grant through raising the rates. In 1981 Labton was placed on the Government's list of authorities which were, by the Conservative Governments' criteria 'overspenders'. Three years later the Government took powers under the Rates Act 1984 to intervene and determine the rate levels of individual authorities or 'cap their rates'. Once the Government had taken the power to prevent councils like Labton from using rate rises to offset the loss of central grant, Labton's financial situation became very serious.

Faced with this new threat the leaders of those Labour authorities likely to be capped concluded that they had to resist the Government on a united basis. Consequently they began meeting together during 1984 to set up a national level campaign against the Government's rate-capping plans. They determined to avoid a situation in which they could be picked off one by one as had happened to Labour councils' opposition to the Conservative Heath Government's 'Fair Rents' Act in 1972–3. In July 1984 the Labour authorities were encouraged by the apparent success achieved by Liverpool City Council in extracting concessions from the Government. Liverpool Council, led by the extreme left 'Militant' faction of the Labour Party, had refused to fix a rate in protest against cuts in central grant and had reached an agreement with the Government involving minor concessions by the latter.

The Labour authorities agreed in the course of 1984 to devise a common strategy of opposition to rate-capping. Briefly there were three possible budget strategies available to local authorities – the 'deficit budget' option , the 'no rate' or 'no budget' option and the 'resignation' option. The first option, the deficit budget option, meant implementing a rate increase within the ceiling set by the Government for the authority but refusing to reduce expenditure and so accumulating a deficit. Of course this option would ultimately bring about an intervention by the District Auditor and very likely lead to surcharges on all councillors who voted for the budget and their being barred from public office for five years. The second option, that of not making a rate but continuing to run services, had already been used by Liverpool. The authority would simply carry on until it ran out of money and was unable to pay its staff or service its debt thus compelling the Government to intervene. The advantage of this option over the deficit budget was that it would bring about a financial crisis earlier as there would be no rate receipts coming in at all. However the chances of personal surcharge and exclusion from office for councillors were just as great as under the first option. The third option was that of resignation so permitting the opposition party or parties to form an administration to carry out the cuts. This option was the least favoured within Labour circles. If the majority Labour group simply resigned the administration and voted out the new minority administration's budget, the situation would be the same as for the no rate option, while to resign and then simply abstain would be pointless as it would permit the Government to get its way over spending cuts and appear as a dereliction of duty by rank-and-file Labour Party members and public service unionists.

In July 1984 the Government announced that seventeen councils were to be rate-capped, sixteen of which were Labour. In the November the Labour leaders determined on a co-ordinated no rate strategy meaning that they were all to make a no rate decision on the same day so presenting a common front of opposition to the Government. At this stage their intention was to threaten and bluff the Government into negotiating with them, though their opposition would appear to have strengthened rather than weakened the Government's resolve to stand firm. To strengthen their position, the sixteen Labour authorities also developed relationships with the local authority unions, the national conferences of which had passed resolutions supporting the non-cooperation with the Government over rate-capping in the Autumn of 1984. These resolutions gave full union support to the Labour employers' opposition to rate-capping, even if such opposition should involve breaking the law.

The financial targets for local authorities over the forthcoming financial year were announced in July and confirmed in December 1984. Labton was expected to spend the same in money terms in 1985–86 as it had in 1984–85 which meant, given a projected inflation rate of 5 per cent, a real spending cut of at least that amount. Moreover Labton, in common with many other authorities had been spending more than was stated in the official figures through the use of 'special funds' – these funds were examples of 'creative accounting' used by authorities to avoid some of the 'clawback' contained in the new system of central grants. It was clear that Labton would have had to make further cuts to remain solvent unless the Government made some allowance for these special funds.

There was even worse news for Labton when the maximum rate levels or caps were announced in December. Labton was given a rate cap more than three per cent below that of the previous year. The council estimated that the impact of the new target and rate limit would mean a swingeing cut of fourteen per cent with an implied loss of 1400 jobs. Clearly such cuts over just one year were far from organisationally let alone politically feasible: it had taken Conborough five years to make comparable cuts. But at this stage Labton did not seek negotiations with the Government in line with the common front agreed by the Labour authorities.

Once the Government targets were known, the local campaign against rate-capping began. The Labton unions had already formed their own campaign earlier in the year, largely on the initiative of one of the NUPE Branch Secretaries. This Labton Joint Union Committee Against Rate-Capping (LJUCARC) included NUPE, GMBATU, TGWU, NALGO and, for the first time, the teaching unions, NUT and NATHFE. LJUCARC followed the national policies of their unions in supporting the no rate option and non-compliance with any officers or agencies seeking to implement rate-capping, policies backed up by the threat of immediate industrial action should any of their members be disciplined for carrying out the policies. LUJCARC also affiliated with a new London-wide organisation, the London Bridge Committee, set up by London local government shop stewards to coordinate local authority opposition to rate-capping and the abolition of the Greater London Council; in fact the Committee was dominated by GLC trade unionists.

In December the Labour Group decided that chairs and other leading members should reassure staff over their futures by visiting departments and explaining their policy to small groups of staff. They began making these visits without prior consultation with the unions. NALGO objected to the lack of union consultation over these visits and some NALGO officials even insisted in sitting in on some of these councillor-staff meetings.

Despite this evidence of distrust from the NALGO leadership, the Labour Group continued with a strategy of cooptation. The main expression of this strategy was the encouragement given to the unions to participate in the various campaigns against rate-capping. The council allocated 100 000 pounds to the campaign in terms of staff and other resources but backed off a union proposal for greatly increased 'time-off' arrangements for unionists to campaign. The unions took advertisements in the local press, the public were leafletted from campaign stalls in the main shopping centres and a 'pledge' circulated inviting staff to pledge their opposition to rate-capping. NALGO held a first ballot of their membership on whether or not the Branch Executive should have the power to put the Union's Industrial Action Rules into operation. This February ballot showed a large majority in favour of industrial action over rate-capping, 73 per cent in favour on a 55 per cent turnout.

In February the then Secretary for the Environment relented slightly and agreed to meet with the leaders of the capped authorities. At the meeting neither side gave any ground, but later the same month the Government issued revised guidelines for five of the capped authorities including Labton. The District Auditor, at Labton's request, had confirmed in writing that the Council's actual level of spending in 1984–85, allowing for the special funds, was higher than the Government had assumed from the published accounts. Accordingly, Labton would have to carry a substantial deficit into 1985–86 for which the Government had made no allowance in calculating the rate and spending limits for Labton. In response to this notification from the District Auditor, the Government lifted the rate ceiling from the original three per cent decrease to an increase of seventeen per cent.

Events moved more rapidly in March. The Labour leaders agreed to hold their budget meetings on the same day (7 March) for maximum publicity and solidarity. On the day before the TUC organised a Day of Action against the cuts in local government jobs and services culminating in a march through central London. In Labton the unions organised a large demonstration of support for the Council and several hundred people marched through the local shopping centre, gathering outside the Council Chamber to hear the proceedings relayed to them over loudspeakers as they munched hotdogs provided by the unions. They heard the Leader of the Council promise that no Council workers would lose their jobs in the course of the forthcoming year but stress that he would not be party to any illegal actions on the part of the Council.

The Council failed to fix a rate at this meeting together with the seven other capped Labour Boroughs. However it soon became clear that the common front among the Labour councils was beginning to crack on the question of whether councils should actually break the law. Early on the morning of 8 March the Greater London Council, the municipal flagship of the London Labour authorities, set a rate well within the Government's limit after a stormy meeting lasting almost twenty-four hours. A few days later the Inner London Education Authority followed. Of course the GLC and ILEA faced a more immediate choice between breaking or staying within the law. As precepting authorities, that is as authorities dependent on the first tier authorities to collect their rates, they were legally obliged to fix their rate twenty-one days before the end of the financial year or face immediate surcharges. In any case the GLC was financially in a very healthy position, making it unnecessary to seek a large rate increase, so that any further opposition to the Government had lost its point. Labton Council met once more during March. The Conservative Opposition called a special meeting of the Council to consider the budget but the Labour Group again used its voting power to defer the rate. At the end of the month the Leader called a special meeting of the Labour Group. By this time it was becoming apparent that the Government was simply going to let events take their course and allow the District Auditor to sort out the errant councils. At the special meeting the Leader gave his view that nothing more was to be gained by further deferrals as the Government was not going to be drawn to the negotiating table. He also brought the Borough Solicitor to the meeting to give the Group the legal option that unless the Council set a rate by the start of the financial year in April, those councillors voting for a further deferral would become personally liable for the costs to the Council of deferral (the cost being mainly the interest on any funds the Council would have to borrow in the absence of rate revenues).

The Leader now argued that the Council should make a legal rate. He gave the meeting two budget options, both of which would protect jobs and services – a 'balanced budget' and 'deficit budget'. Both options involved considerable creative accounting. The first option balanced the budget but meant a rate increase of 17 per cent, the Government's permitted maximum and three times the rate of inflation. The second involved a similar increase of thirteen per cent but implied carrying forward a deficit of almost five million pounds into the next year. Both options assumed that savings of almost 2m pounds could be made painlessly by trimming housing repairs, library expenditure, administrative supports and increasing the vacancy factor. Otherwise notional savings of about 17m pounds were to be made through such creative accounting devices as reducing the Inflation Contingency and the General Contingency Funds, rescheduling the Council's debt and using capital expenditure to reduce revenue expenditure (for example switching non-prescribed capital receipts from the sale of council houses to the Housing Repair Fund).

The Labour Group rejected both options and voted to continue to defer making the rate. The Leader and Deputy Leader resigned immediately as they felt they had lost the confidence of the group. Consequently the Labour group went leaderless into the April Council meeting two weeks later.

The April Council meeting was long and tempestuous. The unions had been lobbying councillors and distributing leaflets declaring that the Council was about to 'bottle out'. The union leaderships were critical of the former Leader's two options. They argued that either option simply meant postponing cuts to the following year. Their fear was that the anti-cuts campaign would lose its momentum so that when the real cuts came, they would be unable to mount an effective opposition. They were also concerned with the loss of credibility among their rank and file they would face it if it turned out that the Council could after all remain within the Government's rate-cap without any job losses.

To maintain pressure on the Labour Group the unions organised a large gathering of unionists which overflowed the Council Chamber into the road outside. Prior to the Council meeting rumours had spread that there would be an attempt to take over the Chamber and physically prevent the meeting from passing a budget; such scenes had already taken place in some other Labour boroughs. Anticipating such trouble the Chief Executive had arranged for extra policemen to be present over and above the usual two. Once the meeting had begun the Labour left objected to the presence of police as intimidatory. The continued presence of police was put to the vote and the Conservative Opposition won with the Labour moderates diplomatically abstaining.

The next issue was whether or not the Borough Solicitor should be permitted to explain the legal position. Again the Labour left objected on the grounds that a political decision had to be taken and questioned the impartiality of the Solicitor. This time the Conservative Opposition and the Labour moderates voted together to hear the Solicitor who again warned the councillors of the dangers of personal surcharge should they continue to defer the rate.

The chief officers had their own budget and rate in reserve. Understandably they were concerned to protect themselves from possible surcharge by ensuring that their warnings on the legality of deferring the rate were clearly registered. The Chief Executive, on behalf of the other chief officers, had explained their position to the leaders of the parties and told them that if an impasse were reached, he would read a prepared statement to the Council on behalf of the chief officers. The statement would have asked the councillors to confirm that the officers had provided them with all the necessary information to make a rate and would have registered the fact that the officers had clearly advised the Council on the legality of the position. The officers would then have presented the Council with their own budget which, in their view, would have led to a satisfactory rate level. In this way the officers believed that they would have demonstrated that they had carried out their responsibilities to the Council should there have been any subsequent judicial review of their actions.

In the event the officers were not required to take up their fallback position. The first motion put to the Council by a centre Labour member that the rate be deferred once again was defeated by an unholy and temporary alliance between the Conservative Minority and the Labour left. The Conservatives took the initiative and proposed their own series of budgetary resolutions, all of which would have meant serious cutbacks, but which were defeated by the Labour Group. Throughout the meeting speakers from the Conservative Minority and Labour moderates had great difficulty in making themselves heard above the barracking from the public gallery and the meeting had to be adjourned several times to eject protestors. By two o'clock in the morning exhaustion was beginning to take its toll. The Conservatives were increasingly anxious about their own position as it was possible that they could be surcharged along with the Labour members as they had already voted down a legal budget. The Labour moderates saw the chance of forming a temporary alliance to push through a legal budget. After some behind the scenes negotiating, the Conservatives and Labour moderates voted together to make a rate on the balanced budget option.

6 Crises of Management Authority

Introduction

Industrial relations has become increasingly adversarial across British local government. The growing pressures of financial stringency and a more intensely ideological form of politics have compounded the problems of policy change through negotiation, whether it be change in the form of retrenchment or policy innovation. This chapter forms a wide ranging discussion of the problems of management in local government during a period of fiscal crisis and the declining feasibility of corporatist strategies, while the two case studies are used to illustrate these problems. The next chapter will complement this discussion by looking at industrial relations problems from the union perspective.

The first part of the chapter considers how policy makers respond to environmental pressures, especially the changing nature of the central-local relationship and of local politics. The second part looks at changes in the negotiability of change, asking to what extent is change still negotiable? and, in particular, the extent to which it is feasible for ruling groups to pursue corporatist strategies; incidentally touching on the question of the legitimacy of unionism in the public services raised by some pluralist writers. Finally the third part looks at how management roles are differentiated in industrial negotiations and in the day-to-day management of departments.

Coping with environmental pressures

Central government and financial restraint

The 1980s were a period of great strain in central-local relations. Local authorities have been seriously affected by a fiscal crisis

created by falling central grants and collectively have opposed the
new systems of financial targets, penalties and rate-capping. Even
many Conservative authorities have questioned the need for such
close central control of their finances. Indeed few authorities have
cut their expenditure to the extent pressed by the Government.
Most authorities have responded with a mixture of spending cuts,
rate increases and 'creative accounting' techniques.

Those authorities that have most opposed central controls and
have been the prime objective of those controls have been Labour.
Those Labour authorities that were rate-capped have responded
to what they perceived as a major encroachment on their
autonomy with a policy of resistance rather than accommodation
to central pressures. The capped authorities across the country
formed a common front and engaged in what one Labour Leader
described as 'a high risk game of poker', risking heavy personal
surcharges on individual councillors and expulsion from office.

Initially the problem in authorities like Labton was seen as that
of managing an external threat to their resource base. But by
early 1985 the problem had become that of the political survival
of local Party leaderships and thus one primarily of internal Party
management: how to hold the Labour Group, the local Party and
the local Labour Movement (including the trade unions) together?
For instance a leading moderate on the Labton group acknowledged that deferring the rate beyond the end of March:

> would not have got the Government to the negotiating table
> but a longer period was needed to convince people of that fact
> within the Party and the local trade unions. It might have been
> possible in a couple of weeks or whatever to convince them
> that there was not going to be any solution but it would have
> been very difficult because attitudes would have hardened but
> at least the logic of it would have become clear.

Inevitably the external threat increased the uncertainties of
management policy and strategy in the capped authorities. Central
government itself compounded these uncertainties by patching
policy together as it went along. The local political leaders themselves were unable to reduce these uncertainties, caught as they
were in a difficult dilemma: if they gave in to Government pressure
too soon their political survival would become doubtful, yet if

they held out sooner or later the resolve of enough of their fellow councillors would fail so forcing them to give in and fix a legal rate.

In the event the tactics of brinkmanship failed to force the Government to the negotiating table. The Government was only willing to negotiate on its own terms as ministers believed that they had nothing to lose by outfacing these Labour councils. Attacks on the 'loony left' as ministers portrayed these councils also had the useful side-effect of distracting attention from continuing severe cuts in government expenditure. Ironically the Labour campaign against rate-capping appears to have been based on the assumption that the very Government they were accusing of right-wing extremism was continuing to play the central-local relations game by the old rules of consensus; whereas the Government itself had long abandoned any other than rhetorical observance of these rules.

Local political management

In municipal elections specifically local issues are usually subsumed in national voting patterns. However the two case studies suggest that councillors are coming to see some industrial relations issues as politically salient. In Conborough the belief that the refuse workers strike would affect the election result did influence the behaviour of key actors. The Conborough Conservatives saw the strike as a potential electoral asset rather than a liability. Perhaps accurately they felt that the public mood had become hostile toward public sector unions and accordingly fought the election on the issue of 'Who governs Conborough? The elected Council or the Unions?' There was a concern within Labour ranks, too, that the strike was electorally disadvantageous to them and the Party distanced itself from the unions during the campaign.

There was also an unusual type of electoral pressure on the Conservatives that had implications for management strategy. Conborough was identified in the media as the vanguard of the new, more radical Conservatism and the leadership felt constrained, after their election in 1978, by a concern to avoid any action that might adversely affect the national prospects of the Conservative Party.

The more serious problem facing party leaderships is that of maintaining their support base in the local party. This problem would seem to be more serious for Labour than Conservative leaders. The Conservative party has traditionally been less factionalised than the Labour Party, while local Conservative Associations have tended to restrict themselves to fighting elections rather than debating policy issues.

In contrast the Labour Party exhibits a greater tendency toward factionalism and over recent years the Party outside the town halls has grown in political significance. Party activists have grown more assertive and attentive to local issues, changes in attitude that have led to a changed relationship between the extra-council Party and Party groups not dissimilar to that between the extra-Parliamentary Party and the Parliamentary Party. There is now automatic reselection of councillors and in some authorities, like Labton, the Leader and main chairs are elected by an electoral college including representatives of the local Party as well as councillors. Local Parties are also routinely represented at group meetings and sometimes coopted onto Council working parties, such as the Labton Decentralisation Working Party, so that senior officers can occasionally find it helpful to deal with key office holders in the Party.

These developments have transformed the task of political leadership. Leaders and chairs now have to be prepared to mobilise support and deflect challenges from the wider Labour Movement as well as from within their Party groups. The growing importance of the former has increased pressures on Party groups to take certain policy lines. It has also limited the freedom of manoeuvre enjoyed by group leaderships in dealing with other parts of the environment, particularly central government. Over rate-capping, for example, the effect of these wider Party pressures was to intensify the rhetoric of confrontation regardless of the political realities. The political leaders were pushed in the direction of confrontation with the Government in a climate in which to doubt that tactic was virtually seen as a betrayal of the Labour Movement itself.

Sustaining the negotiability of change

Tightening financial pressures on councils have increased the problems of negotiating change. The central problem of industrial relations – reconciling the tension between policy change and trust, between managing now and preserving the possibility of managing later – has grown more intractable. The next two sections will consider questions of negotiability in two different contexts: how far can retrenchment be negotiated and what are the problems in negotiating retrenchment? and how far can policy innovations be introduced through negotiation and what are the problems in such negotiations?

How far is retrenchment negotiable?

Where policy makers decide to retrench they have to cope with the inevitable and usually severe strains that organisational cutbacks place on mutual trust between them and the unions. As employers they need to push through policy change without arousing excessive resistance and, in the case of resistance, overcome it without seriously damaging trust. These choices can be summed up in terms of three of the strategies identified in chapter 2 as open to management – cooptation, conciliation and confrontation.

The first strategy, cooptation, has obvious advantages for management. It offers management the possibility of maximising policy achievement while minimising damage to trust and, therefore, avoiding conflict. The drawback of the strategy as a means of retrenchment is that retrenchment itself involves removing incentives for the unions to allow themselves to be coopted. Once the employer begins to remove past material concessions to the unions and to threaten jobs and working conditions, the unions are increasingly unlikely to favour close cooperation. To maintain a cooptative relationship, then, management has to redouble efforts to persuade the workforce that cutbacks are a necessary and inescapable expedient. Such tactics are likely to be more successful in authorities which have been politically stable or have taken a more gradual approach to retrenchment. Such an approach is less likely to arouse an adversarial response than the abrupt introduction of cuts by councils like Conborough. Outside factors are likely to be significant as well such as the state of the local job market, the ideological predispositions of the union leaders and the organisational culture.

Of course Labour as well as Conservative authorities have chosen to retrench. In some authorities the ideological and organisational affinities between the unions and the Party can facilitate cooptation. As the Leader of one Labour authority (not Labton) observed:

> Really we try and carry the unions along with us on all policy issues with which we are involved and, of course, it is more vital than it was before because with public expenditure cuts there are more decisions to be taken that we wouldn't wish to be taken and with a good relationship with the unions we are often able to implement things that we wouldn't if we hadn't that long association.

Under these circumstances the union side comes to share the management's definition of the situation, accepting the decision to retrench as an inevitable adjustment to new economic realities. The effect is to 'depoliticise' the decision, to remove it from the bounds of meaningful debate and, therefore, beyond the scope of bargaining. The propagation of such a definition is considerably assisted by changes in the conventional wisdom which has come to stress the need for financial constraint in the public services.

The second strategy, conciliation, has superceded cooptation in many authorities as relations have grown more adversarial. The change in strategy is typically gradual rather than a single, discrete decision to switch strategy and is produced by an accumulation of decisions, most of which are not primarily industrial relations in content but have industrial relations implications. Nonetheless where retrenchment represents a sharp policy shift with serious implications for employees, the council leadership may anticipate problems and act to forestall any resistance. Certainly the evidence suggests that where retrenching councils have initially not appreciated the extent of resistance and been ill-prepared it was because they assumed that the unions would remain coopted. Only more recently, now that austerity has become the norm, have authorities begun to learn how to cope with the industrial relations fall-out created by retrenchment.

Nevertheless the institutions of industrial relations have a significant role in conflict containment. In Conborough the existence of a developed set of agreed procedures played an important role, acknowledged by management and unions alike, in sustaining a basic level of trust. The disadvantage for management is that such procedures and institutions involve some surrendering of management control – at the very least the unions are given forewarning of management intentions. Such loss of management control concerned the Conborough leadership who felt that the procedures and institutions placed too great a constraint on their freedom of action to achieve their policy objectives. They pressed the unions on a number of occasions to join them in short-circuiting what they saw as ponderous procedures and meetings in favour of small negotiating sessions arranged as and when thought necessary. The unions strongly resisted such a change which they feared would seriously weaken their position. One compromise was the introduction of a negotiating sub-committee of the Joint Staff Consultative Committee which formed a small negotiating forum within the formal structure.

Significantly, despite their sceptical view of the consultative machinery and procedures, the Conborough Conservatives continued to regard any violation of these procedures as a major risk. They recognised the importance of trust and how the institutions sustained trust despite ideological doubts about unionism. Even so they still had to determine the boundaries of the negotiable, that is what issues should fall within the scope of bargaining.

Clearly a retrenching employer faces a dilemma – if consultative procedures are to be meaningful the employer has to allow some issues to be negotiable yet the decision to retrench itself cannot be negotiable. Simply to present staff and union with a cut-and-dried package of cuts is likely to be seen as provocative and as breaking the spirit if not the letter of joint consultation. Accordingly as long as employers determine to avoid confrontation, they try to leave some issues open for negotiation. Yet financial constraint makes it quite difficult for employers to embark on the give-and-take necessary for mutually satisfactory negotiations. Employers simply have too few bargaining chips as the decrement of contraction reduces the possibility of concessions to unions and staff. Almost inevitably retrenching employers come to place duress on the unions implying or even threatening unilateral action unless the unions accept the management case.

Under these circumstances one possible management tactic is to present the unions with a package of cuts greater than that actually intended. Such a tactic has the dual advantage of instilling fear into unions and staff over management intentions while providing the management with some scope to make 'concessions' towards the union. The Conborough Conservatives used this tactic during the 1983–84 Housing Department reorganisation. Initially they indicated their intention to reduce the salaries of those whose posts were downgraded as a result of the reorganisation and only agreed to preserving salary levels after serious staff and union opposition became apparent. Management can use this tactic to achieve their ends while giving the unions the sense that they have achieved some concessions and leaving the staff relieved that the worst has not happened. Of course the use of such a strategy is limited – the more it is used, the less credibility will unions attach to stated management intentions and, therefore, trust management less.

Another possible tactic is to set limits on the extent of projected cutbacks by giving the workforce certain guarantees. The most usual guarantee is that no employee will be made compulsorily redundant and such a guarantee was given in Conborough early in 1982. This guarantee, despite being contentious at the time within the Conservative Group, proved to be a tactically astute move as it reduced the opposition to major staffing reductions. As one leading Conservative commented: 'It was these fears [of compulsory redundancy] that the unions play on so it did have some value in overcoming at a stroke the fear that they were going to be summarily dismissed so it was a necessary expedient.' And Conborough was able to shed a large number of staff through the voluntary severance scheme.

The third management strategy available to a retrenching authority is confrontation. Confrontation does not necessarily mean an overt, provocative attack on the unions, more usually it takes the form of unilateral action contravening agreed procedures. The political leaders turn to confrontation where they believed conciliation involves too great a loss of control to the unions; a perception reflecting the leaders' own perception of what their decision making prerogatives should be. They may anticipate serious opposition and conclude that the formal channels would give the unions the opportunity to delay implementation. Once retrenchment comes to bite into jobs and service conditions rather than just organisational 'slack', growing union resistance makes management acutely aware of the loss of control implied by conciliation.

Confrontation is a high risk strategy. Political leaders do not risk confrontation without believing themselves both in the right and likely to win any ensuing conflict. The Conborough Conservatives held back from unilateral and confrontational action over their first years of office, even being very conciliatory during minor disputes when the unions had anticipated a more confrontational approach. Some leading members were aware of the importance of learning how to cope with union resistance to change. It was only after the first three years that they acquired the confidence, as well as the will, to risk taking on the refuse collectors, the traditional heavy cavalry of the manual unions.

Confrontation can also be covert when it takes the form of attrition. Attrition refers to a situation where the management sets out to weaken the position of the unions through a series of challenges to the unions' position within the local industrial relations system. Management maintains the pressure on the unions over a wide range of issues, yielding minor concessions only in the face of strong union protests even where an issue is not critical to the attainment of expenditure cuts. Furthermore the unions can be weakened through attenuating their resource base – reducing time-off allowances for lay officials, restricting union office accommodation, abolishing the employer deduction of union fees at source and so on.

A final and obvious point is that confrontation destroys trust. To some extent retrenching managements can afford to neglect trust as it is less essential for them than for innovating managements (as will be seen in the following section). Even so trust cannot be completely neglected as a basic level of organisational workability is still required. Thus retrenchment managements use confrontation as an interruption in an otherwise conciliatory strategy and typically endeavour to present it as such to staff and unions.

Is privatisation negotiable?

Privatisation is a means of reducing expenditure through contracting out a discreet area of council activity to private firms. But it involves important and inescapable value questions. The major question is the extent of the responsibility a local authority has or should have for those employed directly on providing council services, Labour and many Conservative councillors still attach considerable value to being 'model employers' and so prefer to find savings through negotiations within the existing industrial relations machinery. Meanwhile other councillors see the debate over privatisation as revolving around the more pragmatic questions of maintaining effective control over a service and improving its efficiency. Those favouring privatisation point to it as a means of reforming restrictive practices of the sort that emerged in refuse collection services toward the end of the 1970s. Thus privatisation enhances management control and consequently enables more effort to be extracted from fewer workers for the same or less pay. In contrast the opponents of privatisation argue that it actually involves a loss of control with potentially long term implications. It replaces a 'worker' monopoly with a 'contractor' monopoly, the latter tending to develop their own abuses unless there is continuing council supervision.

The decision to contract out services is usually presented as an almost inevitable response to union obstinacy and abuses. Certainly in Conborough the Conservatives had little enthusiasm for contracting out early in their administration, less because of ideological reservations and more because it was seen as a high risk policy. They had serious doubts over whether any tenders would be forthcoming and whether they would indeed be competitive with the in-house costs. It was only after the much trumpeted success of another Council, Southend-on-Sea, in putting their cleansing service out to tender that the Conborough Conservatives decided that the risks were manageable.

Privatisation also emerges as a strong policy option when the political leaders conclude that more drastic action is necessary to press on with retrenchment. In Conborough the privatisation decision arose at least partly from genuine Conservative frustration over what they saw as the manual unions' intransigence in negotiations over existing work practices in street cleansing and refuse collection. The Conservatives felt that they had exhausted the possibilities of conciliation and that the unions would only be shifted by a show of determination on the part of the council:

> Privatisation of the cleansing service was just an initial act of desperation. Otherwise, if it hadn't been for the dog in the manger approach of the trade unions, defending the indefensable, we would never have gone as far as we did . . . We were saying . . . that we were just going out to tender to see what the market had to offer. Most of us thought that the street cleansers would mend their ways. The only other alternatives were either to throw money at them and give in to their demands or go out and find out the market price.

The large savings made through privatisation and the defeat of the unions encouraged the Conservatives to press on with the policy. It became a major policy instrument for reducing costs and keeping up the pressure on a public service bureaucracy many of them distrusted:

> We were beginning to lift the lid off the inefficiencies in the service which were being connived at by management . . . I would never accept that you could be sure of getting the best value for money from the Town Hall unless you tested the services by tender. So in July [after the refuse dispute] we decided to test out every service in the market and that has opened the floodgates to a whole shakeout of unproductive labour and cost benefits for the ratepayers as well as a better service.

Is policy innovation still negotiable?

Over the years of post-war growth the unions seldom questioned or resisted policy innovations. Until the late 1970s policy innovations had scarcely to be negotiated as they were additive and associated with incentives to staff compliance such as improved pay and conditions and enhanced white collar career prospects. Professional officers worked for change that was predominantly profession-inspired, professional allegiance and socialisation reinforcing their commitment to such change.

The passing of the years of growth has made innovation more problematical. The fiscal crisis means that policy innovations are now seldom additive but depend on the switching of existing staff and resources, increasing the likelihood of disputes while few incentives are available to sweeten the pill of change. Policy innovations have come to involve tough industrial negotiations. In Labour authorities, and for the most part those authorities that are innovating are Labour, the viability of the traditional Labour strategy of collaboration has declined as authorities have little spare capacity to provide incentives to staff. Consequently authorities like Labton are looking to other strategies to sustain the negotiability of change.

Initially these Labour authorities look towards cooptation. For Labour councillors the difference between collaboration and cooptation often appears slight as they assume that Party-union affinities mean that the unionists share their policy aims. Such assumptions can arise even in the case of NALGO where local Union leaders are seen to be active in local Labour politics and subscribe to left views in their public utterances.

Despite these affinities Labour authorities have encountered union resistance to cooptation. The reasons for this resistance lie in the nature of cooptation as a high trust strategy at a time when political and economic change has begun to undermine the conditions necesary or at least conducive to trust. Trust has been further eroded by uncertainties over future spending plans, reflecting Government policy switches and Labour authorities' vacillations over their own spending. The new guard of Labour councillors have found themselves pursuing new policy initiatives during a period when financial stringency has denied them adequate material inducements for staff cooperation, yet that cooperation has become more vital than ever. Indeed many Labour councillors have begun to recognise the necessity of dampening down staff expectations though ironically the new and ambitious policy commitments of Labour councils tend to fuel these expectations. Of course it is difficult for Labour politicians to abandon the political language of expansionism and endeavour to throw these expectations into reverse, as one senior Labton member wryly observed:

All those years [of growth] were what was known as the good

times in Labton and that included for officers the best possible conditions and highest incremental scales in competing for good officers. Across London, in particular, there was a degree of competition some years ago and over those five years generally everything the trade unions asked for they got. That was easy . . . it was easy to say 'yes' to everything that was being asked for and generally have an easy life. But it also meant that we were almost always saying 'yes' to everything. Now because of the financial stringency we've probably spent most of the year saying 'no' . . . It has been described by both the trade unions and by the Labour Party members this year in terms of employee relations as 'more robust that it was previously'. I thought that was a very polite term. You know it would be nice to have a Labour Government which is going to give us all the rate support grant we need like it used to be. But it isn't going to be the case for the next four years so we're in for a rough old time.

When collaboration and cooptation prove unworkable the main alternative is conciliation. Serious problems of adjustment face Labour councillors in switching to the more adversarial relationship implied. They have to come to terms with their identity as an employer and accept that there is at least a potential conflict of interest between employer and employee despite common membership of the Labour Movement. One senior Chair in Labton expressed his surprise:

It was a real shock to me when it dawned on me, when it became apparent that I was now an employer. I've never wanted to employ anyone in my life, I just don't agree with it but it does come to you fairly early on that the councillors are the employers and the people with whom you sat in meetings with and discussed policies and elections with are suddenly on the other side and they'll say, 'Well, we know that it is not you Mike', and what have you, 'but for these purposes you're the enemy!'

Thus Labour councillors, as happened in Labton, can feel compelled on occasion to take an adversarial stance, however mild, towards their unions in the face of apparent union obstruc-

tion of policy change. As one Labton member complained, in
reference to NALGO boycotts of new posts created in the Economic Development Unit and the Women's Support Unit, 'We get
to the point of implementation of the manifesto and then we don't
get there!' What annoyed members like him was the apparently
opportunistic behaviour of the unions during negotiations over
new policy initiatives. He took the view, as did many of his
colleagues, that the unions saw such initiatives as simply opportunities to put in conditions of service claims. In a similar vein
another senior Labton member expressed his irritation with
NALGO's stance over decentralisation, a stance he thought
exceeded any reasonable definition of their legitimate role as
workplace representatives:

> the initial reaction is one of appallment [*sic*], an appalling atti-
> tude by the trade unions. It is difficult, there are occasions when
> it does appear that the trade unions are fulfilling their duty in
> protecting their members' interest rather more vehemently than
> is absolutely necessary in my view. Having got a sympathetic
> Labour Council there is no need to walk all over it and we
> really ought both to be working for the citizens of Labton.

These types of tension give Labour councillors reasons to consider
confrontation and unilateral action given their concern with policy
change. For example the Labton Labour group dug their heels in
during the Jones dispute which they saw as a test of their authority
as management and as requiring a show of determination in the
face of when was seen as continued NALGO provocation. They
believed that to give in over that dispute would have encouraged
the Union to continue to resist policy change. But for the most
part the Labton leadership avoided confrontation. Political leaders
in innovating authorities, like Labton, tend to recognise the
importance of pursuing high trust relations not just for ideological
reasons but also because such relations are particularly critical to
innovation under constraint. One Labton councillor explained his
and many of his colleagues' stance on industrial relations:

> Industrial relations, it's not about winning and losing, it's about
> losing face and even if you're not an absolute winner with a
> union – you know you sit in there and absolutely crush them

in argument and decision – there's no benefit in that. What you've got to do, like on the Jones issue, is ensure that all parties come out of it with no loss of face or prestige and that is important to people. It might have nothing to do with the issues involved. There's no way to my mind that you make a gain in industrial relations if you crush someone under the table.

In any case conciliation implies a significant distance between the employer and the employed. A distance that is institutionalised as conciliation both involves and is facilitated by the formalisation of negotiating roles and arenas. However where relations become strained the institutions of industrial relations can also come to act as a buffer between the management and the unions, absorbing union pressures on management. In Labton these institutions came to perform such a function as the ruling politicians sought to strengthen these institutions and the role of the Personnel Department, funnelling potential industrial conflict down formally defined channels and away from informal Party-union channels. These channels were strengthened through the accumulation of political decisions within the Labour Group. This accumulation of decisions led to the delegation of authoritative negotiating power to the designated post holders and so reduced the number of points of negotiation (the ways in which increasingly adversarial relations have exposed the inadequacies of informal and ambiguous management roles will be discussed in the next section).

Finally serious dilemmas surround the release and concealment of information. Managements now have to make very careful judgements over what information should be released to unions and at what point in the change process (this is also the case also, of course, where change takes the form of retrenchment). The risks involved in the premature release of information are much greater under present conditions yet the pressure from the unions for information has never been greater. Party leaders are now much more uncertain about their own abilities to deliver on any commitments as they are constrained by declining political stability and limited resources. At best they have just their opinions over likely outcomes to share with the unions. The dilemma is that if they do not share these opinions with the unions they are likely to be accused of excluding the latter from real consultation yet, if they share these opinions with the unions they open themselves to potential misunderstandings – what is intended as an opinion may be taken as hard fact by the unions. Such misunderstandings in the present climate are likely to be construed as management reneging on commitments and lead to a weakening of union trust in management.

Differentiating management roles and responsibilities

The politician as manager

The importance that embattled political leaderships place on the proper differentiation of management roles in sustaining the nego-tiability of change has already been touched upon. This section takes up the question of 'who are the managers?' posed in Chapter 2. The dilemma facing political leaders is that of balancing the pressures to become more involved in 'management' roles with the recognition that industrial disorder can ensue unless a proper differentiation of roles is observed. One aspect of this dilemma is elected members' search for a more satisfactory relationship with senior officer management and another is how to define the nego-tiating role of elected members.

Under the new financial and political pressures councillors have been searching for new ways of structuring their relationships with senior officers as well as with the unions. As long as policy change remained broadly compatible with a high degree of trust, the conventional division of management roles and responsibilities remained workable. Officer management could and did run the organisation with little 'interference' from the elected members. But as high trust and policy change have become less compatible, councillors have taken a greater interest in management activities previously defined as falling within the officer jurisdiction. There are powerful reasons for their closer interest. Councillors are now more concerned to ensure both that senior officers respond to political guidance and, more particularly that the consequences and chances of industrial tensions are contained.

The extent of member control over senior officers is a function of the power structure of the ruling group and the group leaders' perceptions of the particular problem of control before them.

Firstly the ability of a leader or leadership group to control the officer side depends critically on how far power is concentrated in the party group. Leaders able to concentrate power into their own hands within their party group tend to produce a similarly centralised officer structure; while leaders less able to overcome the centrifugal forces of power diffusion have to work with a decentralised, usually highly departmentalised officer structure. The contrasting political leaderships of Conborough and Labton illustrate this tendency for ruling groups to reproduce mirror images of their internal power structure within the officer structure.

Secondly the form of member control is shaped not just by the ideological imperatives of the majority group but also by the perceived organisational obstacles to political direction. For example the need for increased control is likely to be seen as more urgent in an authority where a strongly retrenchment-orientated party has taken over a growth-orientated authority than in an authority that has had a cautious expenditure policy over the years. Conborough is a good example of the former where the Conservatives emphasised the need for control to reverse the 'runaway train' of expenditure against the perceived inertia of an officer structure resistant to cutbacks. The Conservative leadership took very tight control over the financial and staffing aspects of management – through the Staff Review Team they insisted on weekly reports on the finances and levels of employment in the organisation, monitored all replacements of departing staff and designed major departmental reorganisations like that of the Housing Department.

Indeed it has been argued that the concentration of political power is a necessary prerequisite for retrenchment. Such concentration is seen as necessary if the retrenchers are to have the domination necessary to overcome the considerable opposition usually provoked by retrenchment. Certainly the Conborough experience seems to support this line of argument. After they gained power the Conservatives initially approached the problem by opening up the process through a weekend Party Group conference but this exercise was not seen as a success. The Group could agree on cutting politically contentious services created under Labour, such as the community development service and a local arts centre suspected of left ward leanings, but had difficulties allocating further cuts. Similarly the approach of inviting chief officers to come up with cuts for their own departments tended, in the Conservative view, to encourage resistance and delaying tactics. The experience of both the ineffectiveness of the Party Group as a decision making forum and senior officer prevarication convinced the leadership group that they had to concentrate power in their own hands. From then on the task of retrenchment was carried through by meetings of the key committee chairs and particularly through the small but powerful Staff Review Team.

The concentration of political power in this way is not always as feasible, even in Conservative authorities, as it was in Conborough. As was pointed out in Chapter 2 the current trend is for power in party groups to become less concentrated. Where power is diffuse, the council leader and other chairs are less able to take the initiative in the way they did in Conborough. They are likely to find the task of retrenchment more difficult as other members fight for their own pet services and to keep cuts away from ther own constituents, as local pressure groups sway members and as chief officers press the case for their departments by briefing chairs and other sympathetic members.

Similarly leadership problems in achieving policy innovation occur where power is diffused within the ruling party. In Labton the major reason for delays in the implementation of new policy initiatives such as decentralisation and equal opportunities was the absence of a focused political will behind these initiatives.

Recent political changes have also had important implications for chief officer management teams. Many elected members have come to suspect these teams of usurping their own power, an attitude that has led to moves to limit the power of these teams. In Conborough the Management Review Team reduced the importance of the management team while the latter felt less able to make decisions on industrial relations matters which had acquired too great a political sensitivity. In Labton, too, the management team became more marginalised as leading members doubted senior officers' support for their political aims.,

The politician as negotiator

The elected politicians have become more involved as negotiators with the unions than was the case previously. Politicians now see union relations as more critical to successful policy implementation and distrust the abilities of chief officers as negotiators and as trouble shooters able to contain situations where even minor disputes (like the Jones dispute) can flare up into major conflagrations. Industrial relations bargaining has grown in importance when resource constraints are severly limiting the employers' ability to offer concessions. One consequence is that senior officers are experiencing greater difficulty in acting as authoritative negotiators. They are forced to make frequent reference back to the political leadership as financial constraint has made even minor concessions matters of political decision and created tensions that increase the likelihood of disputes flaring up. Indeed many officers now prefer the members to front up negotiations.

The emergence of elected members as fully fledged negotiators is closely associated with the shift towards conciliation. Under cooptation and collaboration their role as negotiators remains undeveloped and less important. However to be effective conciliatory strategies require authoritative negotiators. The designated negotiators must have the necessary delegated power and political latitude to negotiate authoritatively – that is, to make agreements with the minimum of reference back to other members and with the requisite political authority within the group to guarantee political approval of agreements.

The emergence of such authoritative negotiators requires a basic level of political stability within the majority group. Where such stability is absent, usually where power is diffuse, the formulation and maintenance of consistent management policies and strategies becomes a serious problem.

Persistent failures by management to negotiate consistently reduce management-union trust. Union negotiators who experience inconsistency on the part of their management counterparts tend to grow cynical of the ruling party's willingness or ability to honour agreements. Moreover, when there is so much uncertainty over the political commitment, they develop consequent doubts over entering into negotiations over new policy innovations. Another important consequence of political instability is the tendency for members of the ruling group to open up their own points of negotiation with the unions; a tendency more typical of Labour than Conservative authorities but by no means confined to them. Early on in Labton these informal negotiations were a particular problem and formed one reason for the increased formalisation of industrial relations, which meant a curtailment of these informal points of negotiation in favour of one formal, politically sanctioned point of negotiation.

Usually the personnel chairs constitute the formalised point of negotiation. Their political importance has increased over recent years but again their authority depends on the power structure of the group. Where that structure is concentrated and stable, personnel chairs are much more likely to be able to negotiate freely and authoritatively than where that structure is diffuse and unstable. In the former case the chances are lower both of their being over-ruled by their political colleagues and of the latter opening up their own points of negotiation. But personal qualities should not be forgotten. More successful personnel chairs have learnt how to anticipate both the likely responses from their group as well as those from the unions and so are able to act with some independence of their group. For instance the Conborough Personnel Chair who had negotiated the early severance scheme stressed the need to operate at some distance from the Party Group and to minimise the importance of 'report back': 'I think it would be fair to say that I negotiated with the unions first and told my Party afterwards . . . if I was going to talk to a union man, if was off the cuff and never went back to anybody and there were meetings that no-one [in my Party] ever heard of.'

Broadly personnel chairs experience greater difficulty in maintaining the necessary political authority in a Labour than in a Conservative Council. Labour groups are characterised by greater power diffusion and factionalism than Conservative groups, though by no means all Conservative leaderships can engineer the stability and centralise power to the extent that the Conborough leadership managed. Labour chairs have the further difficulty of coping with the informal points of negotiation as, for example, happened in Labton during the Porters' Strike. To be effective Labour chairs have to manage the local political system as well as the industrial relations system.

Relations between personnel chairs and other leading members are not without strains. In the new tough industrial relations climate personnel chairs require the support of political colleagues yet are more likely than ever to be encroaching on the departmental baronies of other chairs. One former Labton personnel chair remarked on the way in which he had become involved right across Council departments: 'One thing I never realised on taking the job was whoever makes errors causes problems – problems with the unions, with individual personnel, with other officers – all of these problems come across the Council to me. We span all the services. I didn't realise that you had to pick up every other ball.'

He continued by arguing that he had had to be aware of 'the global position of the Council – where it might be possible to trade in one issue in one committee for an issue in another to achieve things. That's how I've always operated, call it wheeling the dealing if you like but that's the game we are in to.' Such a global role is seen as necessary in many authorities, such as Labton, given the tightening of resource constraints. Negotiations in any one department have to be conducted with an awareness that a badly considered settlement can create a series of leap-frogging claims across departments with financial implications not easily absorbed within existing budgets. Similarly departmental disputes and individual grievances can spread rapidly unless they are picked up quickly and resolved. The industrial relations game is now a complex one where trade-offs are made right across all fields of council activity and so requires powerful players able to play right across the board of council services.

Significantly the Labton leadership looked to institutionalisation to bolster their authority as negotiators, in particular to reduce the number of informal points of negotiation. The leading members recognised that the proliferation of negotiating points seriously weakened the authority of officer management. In their view the unions had almost automatically escalated disputes to member level, bypassing officer management and so removing the latter's effective powers of negotiation. As one former personnel chair explained:

This is why the officers lost confidence going way back, the officers had no confidence in handling industrial disputes because unions, particularly the manual unions, would get to the members within the confines of the Party. The next day the members would pull the rug out from beneath the officers. What the members in this authority now know is that before the unions can do anything like that they have to get by me . . . that is totally realistic.

Another leading member similarly stressed:

> All negotiations should be taken in front of officers and there
> is none of this 'Let's go down to the pub and sort things out
> over the bar' . . . then next morning the officer comes in and
> believes one thing and the chaps come in and say, 'We've got
> an agreement on this'. In this way you are weakening your
> whole management structure, if you're going to have credibility
> you should not weaken your management structure.

These remarks point to a growing awareness of how management
weaknesses have emerged under new pressures and also to the
value to members and officers of clearly differentiating management roles. Leading members also began to learn that there were
possible advantages to being distanced from involvement in staff
management and more minor industrial disputes. The leading
figures in Labton favoured a clear hierarchy of management roles,
one former personnel chair argued that the personnel chair should
be 'three times removed, there is the service [department], there
is Personnel and me if that is necessary'. He regretted that he had
continued to be drawn into disputes that should have been handled
at departmental level. Similarly he and his colleagues thought that
as elected members they had allowed themselves to be pulled into
the Jones dispute too early on. If they had held back longer they
might have avoided being identified with the hard line taken by
the Direct Works management. If NALGO had seen the members
as more independent then, they might have agreed to a member-
level review of the case before the strike had become so
widespread.

The quality of personal relationships between management and
union negotiators is also important. A good working relationship
can help preserve trust through difficult and contentious negotiations. Negotiations are usually assisted when the negotiators
share some confidences with the other side. To some extent this
happened in Conborough where one personnel chair shared his
political difficulties in selling agreements back to his Group with
the union negotiators. Such an approach can have the useful side-
effect of encouraging the unions to settle early with an apparently
moderate management negotiator rather than risk the involvement of less sympathetic councillors.

Finally management negotiators have to cope with other sources of potential distrust. One source can be a vacillating and changing negotiating stance by union negotiators. Such vacillation may reflect the problems of leadership instability within the union itself as much as any manoeuvring for advantage. In Labton, for example, Labour members complained about what they saw as NALGO's shifting stance in negotiations. Some Labour members appeared unwilling to make allowances for any internal political problems the Union might have been experiencing. They were unhappy with the style and content of NALGO policies and, more generally, the new generation of local government officers with whom they identified the then NALGO leadership. One leading member complained of the 'campus politics' introduced by this new generation:

> I see it as nothing more than zealots or young bucks, call them what you may, coming into Labton and wanting to reintroduce their campus politics into the situation. It goes beyond that, I don't mean just in terms of trade unions, you can get a bevy of social workers into a place like Labton where they go onto the Council estates and want to regiment the pensioners because it is the right thing to do. They want to try and recreate a whole bloody campus on a council estate. That may be totally wrong but that is how I perceive it.

This view was related to a concern that these officers were becoming politically active in the Labour Party: 'Call it a degree of entryism if you like, but yes, they are widening their sphere of influence'. The Conborough Conservatives harboured similar doubts about their union leaders. In line with some pluralist approaches, they certainly saw their unions as using industrial muscle to pursue 'political' rather than 'industrial' ends, as one Conservative observed: 'There were tremendous pressures on the workforce to make them take action on behalf of wider interests'.

The officer as manager

This final section turns to the problems arising from the mediating role of chief officers caught between the ruling party and the officer structure. They have to reconcile the policy expectations of the politicians with growing organisational intractability as staff become less receptive to authority and managerial direction. Thus chief officers face a growing dilemma of having to respond rapidly to political direction while that political direction is itself a threat to their own good staff relationships. In other words the more that the policy objectives and, therefore, the interests of the ruling politicians and staff diverge, the greater become the problems for chief officers of maintaining trusting relations with departmental staff.

In retrenching authorities chief officers are having to switch from planning service expansion to planning, insofar as it is possible, the orderly decline of services. The Conborough chief officers were very aware of this major change, one described his sense of 'an absolute change in attitude in Conborough since 1978, the like of which you would probably not find anywhere else in local government . . . we've privatised many things, we've cut to a degree few other authorities have, reduced staff by a thousand since 1978. It is a dramatic and different experience'. In a similar vein another chief officer referred to the 'severe problem of adjustment from the days when we were going to spend, spend, spend. The problem is that since then I have not been able to do anything that I would describe as the work of a chief officer, you're far too involved in pleading and arguing every individual problem'.

Even in authorities that remain growth-orientated chief officers face comparable problems in meeting high member expectations. One Labton chief officer expressed his amazement at the demands for 'instant management' thrown up by the ideological ferment of Labton:

> The reaction to things that happen in this community has undoubtedly changed. I refer to it as 'instant management'. If something happens tonight, we will probably have a meeting about it at two or three o'clock. By the following morning action will have been expected. By the following evening people will say, 'Well, we decided that' as if it were ages ago, 'What has happened? Has enough been done about it?'

Chief officers face an especially difficult conflict of loyalties when the ruling politicians decide on a course of confrontation. Where management and unions become polarised, the ruling group expects their chief officers to take the management side and abstain from industrial action, while the staff and unions expect them if not necessarily to join any action at least to distance themselves from the ruling group. In practice chief officer NALGO members are reluctant to take action because of the danger of being compromised in the eyes of the elected members. Those Conborough chief officers, for example, who joined the picket lines during a one day strike against the cuts in 1981 experienced considerable Conservative anger at their public display of 'disloyalty'. It does take considerable political skill and judgement for chief officers to cope with the conflict of loyalties and retain the trust of both sides.

The more usual problem for chief officers is how to avoid being too closely identified with policies which their staff regard as threatening to their jobs and service conditions. Too close an identification may weaken their managerial authority, staff being less willing to comply with managers who no longer appear to share their values. Such a difficulty is especially acute where chief officers come under intense member pressure to endorse policies of privatisation and service cutback. Comparable problems also occurred in those authorities which opposed central government over rate-capping. In Labton the chief officers found themselves identified with central government after advising caution to a ruling group and union leadership bent on confrontation with the Government. In the words of one chief officer: 'the implications were that the officers had played a part that they shouldn't have played in the sense that they appeared to be acting as establishment creatures'.

Chief officers can resort to various strategies to reduce their chances of being identified with certain policies by their staff. An important and obvious strategy is to share information with the staff but this strategy can create member distrust of the officers, one chief officers explained:

> Staff come to me and ask, 'How much are you keeping to your chest?' And I say, 'That's OK but on the times I have shared things with you it gets leaked out at the wrong time and is more likely to hinder than to help . . . so I am going to carry on as I have been because it simply drives the members into a corner and they get nasty'. So early on I thought that I would have to

be careful which is a major change. I would like to be more communicative with staff and I think that is more a feature of most authorities.

Finally chief officers face particular difficulties where power is diffused within the majority group and chairs lack authority among their colleagues. These problems are further compounded by the emergence of 'policy networks' linking councillors and staff. These networks should be carefully distinguished from the traditional collaborative relationship. Unlike the latter these policy networks have a strong policy content, are not union based and typically involve white rather than blue collar workers. Whereas collaborative relationships are far more characteristic of blue collar workers and are centred on pay and conditions issues, these networks have wider implications for chief officers as managers. One Labton chief officer explained:

> Labton does not operate as a hierarchy anymore, there is contact at all levels between the officers and the officers, between members and the officers. That is going on all the time so that a Leader or a chair may make his contact on a particular subject at a much lower level than that of chief officer. That again is a cause of conflict because people are very busy and sometimes a chief officer might be told that there has been contact between that particular member and someone in the department and the first you know of it is some manifestation of that discussion. That can be annoying at one extreme and dangerous and certainly difficult at another.

Another chief officer stressed the consequences of these contacts for staff relations. He complained of how 'the normal machinery and process can be gone through and yet another effort is made in different directions to put pressure on me and the management'. In his view the networks meant that senior managers could not rely on the automatic support of the elected members. Consequently 'the attitude of management [in his department] is a very firm one – unless the members are prepared to support us, we will not do anything [during industrial disputes]'. He stressed that he and his managers had to anticipate and, if possible, avoid any situations in which the members were put in the position of having to back him up as director against the unions.

However, particularly over authority-wide industrial issues, senior Labton officers did report an improvement from increased institutionalisation. One chief officer described the evolving state of affairs: 'the automatic thing was to escalate everything to the members so that what [the unions] had done was to take the bargaining strength out of my level – I could say "no" but they wouldn't accept that unless it was to their advantage. They are doing now because they realise that if they go to the members they might get "no" as well.' He thought that it was essential 'to keep the rope tight, it doesn't mean that you've got to block everything but you certainly do *not* have to provide an escape route higher up otherwise they will go for it'. The rapidity with which NALGO took the Jones dispute to member level illustrates the tendency of unions to use all such available 'escape routes'.

7 The Unions and the Management of Discontent

Introduction

The problems of change are far from being solely a management concern. Union leaders have also to cope with the problems arising from the fiscal crisis. Now that the earlier corporatist type relationship is breaking down, they have to search for a middle way between too much confrontation and too much collaboration with the employer (see Chapter 3). This search involves the major tasks both of responding effectively to management policies and strategies and also of managing discontent within the local union organisation. The focus of this chapter is on these tasks. The first section examines the tasks and problems of responding to policy change in the forms both of retrenchment and of policy innovation; in particular it considers the spreading rejection of employer collaboration by the unions. The second section considers the complications that management differentiation and fragmentation introduces into the management-union relationship. While the third section looks at the changing problems of union leadership in terms of the management of discontent.

Responding to change

Retrenchment

The decision to retrench takes different forms open to varying intrepretations by the unions. As was stressed in the last chapter employers may anticipate opposition and modify their intentions accordingly. In any case the transitional period from growth to retrenchment, as in Conborough, typically takes the form of a 'phoney war'. The threat of cutbacks appears to unions and staff as rhetorical rather than real as early cuts are in future plans and organisational slack. Union leaders have to interpret both the words and the actions of the employer to anticipate the moment when retrenchment will become a real threat. Once they have established the employer's intention to retrench, the choices facing local union leaderships can be understood as being among confrontation, collaboration or conciliation.

In many authorities the unions have continued to collaborate with the management rather than adopt a more adversarial stance. In part this continuing attachment to collaboration reflects the timing of cutbacks. Councils as employers are aware of the import-ance of timing expenditure cuts. Union leaders and members are more likely to perceive a sudden switch in council policy from growth to retrenchment as threatening (especially following a change in political control), than a more gradual transition to retrenchment. Sudden cutbacks, as occurred in Conborough, are usually seen as provocative by the unions. Another significant factor is the mobilisation of bias favouring collaboration that builds up over the years in an authority and precludes the emerg-ence of a more adversarial view of the relationship. Such a bias appears particularly characteristic of authorities in rural or outer suburban areas where workforces remain less militant than their counterparts in urban areas.

During retrenchment employers try to reinforce any such organ-isational bias. Union leaders are subject to strong management pressures to accept cutbacks as an inevitable adjustment to outside financial pressures and, moreover, an adjustment sanctioned by their electoral mandate. Of course the general climate of public sector stringency created by central government eases the task of persuasion. Union leaders in many authorities have indeed accepted the inevitability of retrenchment. Such an acceptance may be simply pragmatic – the union has no choice but to coop-erate – or as normative – reflecting the leaders' willingness to accept the employer's definition of the situation. Normative acceptance is more likely where the employer is trusted to main-tain at least existing jobs. Many Labour authorities have reduced their expenditure with the cooperation of local unions, ironically the organisational and ideological affinities between a ruling Labour Party and the unions can enhance trust and so facilitate union acceptance of the employers' definitions.

In contrast unions are more likely to resort to confrontation where they anticipate or are encountering a threat to their past achievements in terms of jobs or service conditions. The unions often turn to confrontation where they are experiencing what they see as confrontational action on the part of the employer. In particular the decision to retrench, even if in itself it is not seen as confrontational, may well produce employer action of a confrontational type. The union leaders and membership respond to that decision according to how they perceive the type of cut – cuts in existing job holders being the most threatening. The method of introducing cuts also influences union perceptions of the extent of the threat. Cuts introduced in a low trust way – outside the formal and agreed channels and without prior warning – are more likely to be seen as threatening than cuts proposed in a high trust way – through the formal channels and with prior consultation.

Thus confrontation represents an attempt by a union to veto a course of action on which the employer has embarked. As such it involves a withdrawal of consent by the workforce to the employer's policy objectives, typically taking the form of a threat of industrial action followed, if the threat has been unsuccessful, with the actuality of industrial action. However, as will be seen later in this chapter, confrontation depends crucially on the ability of the union leaders to mobilise their members. Given the ever-present possibility that management may call the union's bluff, it must be recognised as a high risk strategy as any failure to back up a threat of industrial action with the reality inevitably weakens the bargaining credibility of union leaders.

The main danger is that the employer might hold out in the face of industrial action. As was argued in Chapter 1 (against the pluralists Wellington and Winter), the public service employer is in a stronger position to ride out such action than a private sector employer, especially where the former attaches little importance to averting a political crisis arising from industrial relations. Ironically the success of industrial action or threatened action depends on the willingness of the employer to maintain a basically concili-atory strategy towards the union. In Conborough the first four major disputes involving industrial action were largely successful, in union terms, because the Conservatives at the time remained basically conciliatory. Later on over the privatisation question the Conservatives determined that the principle of outside tendering

was not negotiable and so they abandoned their earlier conciliatory approach. Meanwhile the unions failed to realise that the
Conservatives' commitment to the policy of privatisation by then
overrode any commitment to mutual trust.

The effectiveness of strike action or threatened strike action, it
will be recalled from Chapter 3, depends on the strategic location
and substitutability of workers, both of which vary widely among
groups of workers. Strategic location refers to the ability of a
group of workers to impose heavy costs on the employer. For
example the refuse collectors have historically enjoyed considerable industrial power because any strike action rapidly created a
political crisis with the accumulation of refuse and consequent
public outcry and risk to public health. In addition their high
degree of worker solidarity and councils' unwillingness (for
reasons of cost) to bring in contractors meant they had low substitutability. However in Conborough the strategic location of the
refuse collectors proved to be a wasting asset. The Council had
the means of substitution close at hand in the form of the company
already undertaking the street-cleansing as well as a strong
political commitment to take risks in breaking the power of the
manual workers.

Unskilled manual workers are especially vulnerable to substitution as the rapid replacement of the Conborough refuse collectors by private contractors illustrates. Consequently the cooperation of the white collar workers, who were both strategically
located and less easily substitutable, was important in increasing
the effectiveness of the action. Although, in turn, the effectiveness
of the white collar selective action was reduced when the Council
brought in substitute agency staff to run the switchboards.

In general white collar workers are less vulnerable to substitution, usually being more skilled (or at least seen to be so) than
manual workers. Many also have skills specific to local government employment, unlike even their skilled manual counterparts,
so that substitute staff cannot easily be taken from the private
sector to replace striking staff. However white collar staff, such
as social workers and teachers, can have ambiguous strategic
locations in the sense that the effectiveness of any action depends
on how the employer perceives the consequences in political
(especially electoral) and normative terms. Thus the seriousness
with which councillors view threats of action by street-level

bureaucrats, such as social workers and teachers, depends on their level of concern for the clients and service users. Other white collar officers, particularly those in financial areas, have a more clear-cut strategic location as they are able to impose severe costs, financial and otherwise, on the employer.

The appreciation of the potential power of white collar staff deters ruling politicians from making direct threats to their job security. In Conborough the Leader of the Council learnt the hard way through the NALGO response to the threat of compulsory redundancies when he made his threat of 700 redundancies. As one NALGO official mused: 'They are still very nervous, surprisingly, about the white collar staff's reactions. They always want to know "if we can do this? What do you think might happen?" If they get a strong rebuff, they are willing to rethink – at least up to now.'

Unions can compensate for limitations to their strategic location and substitutability in further ways. One way is through the formation of outside alliances with user or consumer groups, and such alliances have been a growing feature of union resistance to expenditure cutbacks (in line with the fiscal crisis thesis). These alliances have significant advantages in preventing a council's attempts 'to marginalise the trade unions'. Direct action by users increases the effectiveness of industrial action or even obviates the need for such action. The dispute over the housing privatisation feasibility study in Conborough illustrates the tactical value of such alliances for unions. NALGO was able to win the dispute as a result of the picketing activites of the tenants associations despite Union members' reluctance to take action in the face of severe disciplinary threats from the employer. Moreover consumer involvement strengthens a union's case against cutbacks as it counters the argument that the unions are simply defending their narrow employment interests. Such alliances also threaten politically embarassing situations such as councillors facing protests by service users.

The Conborough case underscores the need for an effective confrontational strategy to be prepared and planned carefully. Union leaderships have not only to consider the factors of strategic locations and substitutability but also to anticipate the likely reaction on the part of the employer. Conborough NALGO Branch leadership prepared carefully for what they saw as the inevitable showdown with the Council. Soon after the Conservatives came to power the union leadership began building up a strike fund and preparing plans for selective action: 'all through this time we were very conscious that we were going to be facing compulsory redundancies at some point so this exercised our minds more than anything else. . . . Everything we were doing was based on the idea that we had to organise our members for long and serious industrial action'.

Confrontation is a prelude to conciliation as ultimately it is intended to bring employers to the negotiating table or to strengthen the union bargaining position. Even in Labour councils union leaders have turned from collaboration towards conciliation as retrenchment has cut into jobs and working conditions. Conciliation involves a strong emphasis on the protective function of industrial relations institutions. Thus the Conborough unions attached considerable importance to institutional structures and formal agreements – the NALGO Branch, in particular, anticipated the Conservative takeover and obtained major procedural agreements during the last years of Labour rule.

Even within a broadly conciliatory strategy, union leaders face a difficult dilemma. Retrenchment poses them a difficult choice between too much confrontation and too much collaboration. Too much collaboration means smoothing the way for cutbacks and so can be seen as encouraging the employer to continue with further retrenchment policies. Moreover collaboration involves major concessions for the union without any equivalent compensating advantages. At best some collaboration can be seen as staving off the worst cutback scenarios which, in Conborough for example, simply meant preserving job security when the unions decided to cooperate after the threat of 700 redundancies in 1982: 'We cooperated with the cuts, with the job loss and in return our members got security of job and many of them got higher grades.' Collaboration at that point in Conborough, then, was seen as averting the threat of compulsory redundancies and actually gaining some minor advantages in terms of staff regradings.

Nevertheless some confrontation would seem to be necessary to prevent the employer from interpreting reluctant cooperation as acquiescence or even as consent. In Conborough union collaboration did not occur until after confrontation had convinced the Conservative leadership that any compulsory redundancies would be hard fought. Especially where unions distrust management, they have to ensure that the management are aware of the likely cost to them of any policy change in terms of industrial disruption. Yet long campaigns of confrontation against cuts are futile and can even be counter-productive, as one union official commented: 'Up to now my ambition was never to be King Canute but to build boats!'

Policy innovation

Policy innovation under conditions of no growth creates a more difficult and ambiguous situation for unions than retrenchment. As was argued in Chapters 2 and 3, as long as conditions of growth persisted policy innovation was seldom a problem as new policies were additive and associated with enhanced rewards for staff, while professionalism reinforced the basically consensual nature of change. Now that the increment of growth is no longer available, policy innovation has become more of a problem for unions.

In many Labour authorities unions have come to assume that the employer will continue to collaborate with them. However, as was shown in the last chapter, employer collaboration with the unions (or union cooptation of the employer) is ceasing to be viable. The search for savings and the pressures for policy change have intensified across authorities and disrupted any collaborative relationships. Instead the employers are demanding greater employee willingness to cooperate and expecting themselves to coopt the unions in the implementation of their new and radical policy programmes.

In response the unions can allow themselves to be coopted by their employing councils or, in other words, collaborate with the employer. Collaboration means smoothing the way for the employer to introduce policy change. The drawback for the unions is that they must forgo major opportunities to extract concessions from the management. Union leaders face a dilemma here especially where they regard the outcome of a projected change to be desirable in terms of either improved work practices or their own more partisan political aims. Indeed there may even be some pressures within the local union branches for collaboration from those union members who support the local Party programme. A good example (not mentioned in Chapter 5) of such pressures for a collaborative approach was the equal opportunities policy in Labton where NALGO took the initiative in pressing the Council to reduce indirect racial discrimination by advertising posts outside the Council staff.

However if unions cooperate or collude with one policy innovation, they reduce their ability to negotiate over later changes. In other words they cannot afford to neglect process in favour of policy outcomes (see Chapter 3). Consequently union officials typically insist on negotiating over even 'agreed' policy changes because they see a need to defend agreed process. Thus the Labton union leaders made it plain that they intended to contest even quite minor changes. One manual union official described how he kept up the pressure on management to stick to the letter of agreements by protesting even over minor matters, such as the otherwise uncontroversial replacement of a petrol pump by management without prior consultation.

Conciliation, then, is becoming the dominant strategy where unions are working with innovating councils even on the left. The new stress on the process and institutions of industrial relations is shared by local unions in innovating as well as in retrenching authorities. The new politics of austerity have made the unions very aware of the benefits of greater formalisation, in the words of a former NALGO Branch official:

I think the business that we were in was to extend the extent to which we had a role in decision making within the organisation and I think we did that to some extent. We got a whole range of agreements with the Council on procedures which meant that they were compelled to consult the trade unions on changes that they were about to make, for example something that was started when I was Branch Secretary was [consultation over] changes to office acommodation.

There must be serious questions about the capacity of these formalised industrial relations structures to cope with negotiations over complex policy initiatives such as decentralisation. The primary function of the joint consultative committees is consultative rather than participative, their main function being that of a forum in which the staff side are consulted over changes already worked out by management. They are poorly suited to the partici-

pation of unions and staff in the formulation and implementation
of policy initiatives, while procedureal agreements on matters such
as staff redeployment can actually further impede participation.

Perhaps surprisingly union leaders themselves accept and inter-
nalise this organisational bias towards a constrained role for
unions. Certainly in Labton they defined their role in reactive
rather than in proactive or participative terms. They felt more
comfortable in the traditional reactive role and were very wary of
taking on a more proactive role. On decentralisation the NALGO
leaders refused to join joint working parties on the issue and
instead insisted that they would only negotiate when the Council
came up with some concrete proposals. They wanted to bargain
rather than participate: 'We've said all along that we'll discuss it
with you [the Council] if you come along with your plans and they
haven't done that. We won't have piecemeal decentralisation but
when you have an overall plan come and talk to us about it.'

Behind this continuing attachment to a reactive role there can
be a concern that participation really means cooptation by the
employer. In Labton such a view was reinforced by some scepticism of the Labour Group's continuing commitment to decentralisation and doubts about the wisdom of incurring major expenditure on decentralisation at a time when jobs could be at risk.
Nevertheless most union leaders in Labton were insistent that the
proper role of a union, even in a Labour authority, was to bargain
with the employer over service conditions issues and not to play
a more proactive role.

Rate-capping

The problems facing local union organisations in authorities like
Labton are compounded by the environmental pressures on the
employing authority. Almost inevitably the unions become
entangled in the debates over how the authority should respond
to the financial pressures imposed by the Conservative central
government. In Labton Labour councillors wooed their support
and warned of serious consequences if staff and council failed to
make a common front against the Government. Many leading
union activists also identified with the Council's struggle against
a Conservative Government in the polarised political climate
created by the Thatcher Government during the 1980s.

In the face of the external threat of rate-capping local union leaders opted for collaboration. Many union activists argued that the unions had no option but to collude with the Council. If they had been critical of the Council's approach they believed that they would have had difficulty selling their members a stance critical of an employer apparently intent on saving services as well as weakening the Council's stand against the Government, the real villain of the piece. Furthermore the ideological sympathies of many union activists inclined them towards the stance adopted by the left faction within the Labour Group.

In the event the union leaders felt let down over what they saw as the Labour Group's failure to bring them into their confidence and inner counsels as the political crisis of rate-capping unfolded. Certainly in this case the unions saw collaboration as involving a partnership with the politicians and expected the latter to share details of their intentions with them. Meanwhile the latter, for the reasons outlined in Chapter 6, were not and did not feel able to share information and plans with them. Consequently the union leaders felt that they were being given rhetorical promises about what the Labour Group intended, promises that they felt would or could not be upheld under the pressure of events, as one union leader observed: 'The problem we have with this Council is that they say one thing and then go and do another and I've no confidence in the public statements they make so I don't think that this Council will adopt a Liverpool type approach.'

When the Leader of the Labour Group finally produced a legal budget, many union leaders reported a sense of being let down. They had campaigned among their members on the basis of an imminent crisis in Labton's finances, implying at least 2000 redundancies, yet suddenly Labton was able to maintain its employment level within a legal budget. The union leadership saw this outcome as having 'effectively pulled the rug from underneath our campaign'. As a result the union leaders felt that they had lost credibility with their members: 'By becoming so closely identified with the Council's campaign, the debacle has weakened our members' confidence in the Union as well as the Council'. In retrospect several union leaders concluded that it would have been better if 'everyone had been honest about their position' from the first.

Relating to management

The ruling party

Fragmented management considerably complicates the tasks of union leadership in responding to management policies and strategies. It also complicates the tasks faced by union leaders in industrial relations negotiations, giving rise to both opportunities and problems for union leaders. In particular union leaders have to consider the pattern of power distribution within the ruling group.

The diffusion of power within a party group produces conditions under which union negotiators can open alternative, informal points of negotiation and even discover the bargaining stance of the employer. During disputes or in the lead up to disputes union leaders have to decide with whom to negotiate, over what type of issue and at what point in the development of a dispute. There is a temptation to go straight to the elected members early on in a dispute over the heads of the officer management, a particularly strong temptation in Labour authorities because of the organisational and ideological affinities. Such direct union-member contact is not unknown in those Conservative authorities where increasing factionalisation has produced politicians willing to talk with the unions behind the backs of their leaderships though, in the case of Conborough, union attempts to make such contact were almost invariably unsuccessful, mainly because of Party discipline and solidarity.

Historically collaborative employer strategies have encouraged such contact, though mainly in the case of manual rather than white collar unions. But as employers have adopted more conciliatory strategies, such informality has been superseded by a new emphasis on the use of formal channels and a hierarchy of managerial negotiating roles. The Labton unions, then, found the informal channels increasingly closed off to them especially as the Labour Group developed a greater sense of group cohesion (until the political crisis over rate-capping). Leaders in the manual unions, traditionally the main users of informal channels, reported that they were using them less and were taking issues to officer management. This change in approach had largely arisen from their experience of increasingly futile contacts with the members as the latter were no longer able to make concessions towards the unions (as was seen in the last chapter).

This choice between informal and formal contacts can be further illustrated by reference to the Labton NALGO Branch. Within the Branch there were differences between the advocates of increased informality and the advocates of formality. One former NALGO official, an advocate of informality, described his approach:

> We were beginning to develop an approach of 'we've got a problem, let's sort it out, we don't need reports, we don't need to go through the joint structure' and in that way we were beginning to operate in a very similar way to the manual workers who operate in that way all the time. They will literally bust a door down to straighten something out with a chief officer or whoever.

In contrast his successors were critical of his direct and informal approach: 'I don't know that horse trading behind the scenes actually does any good. I think that there is a tendency to think that you should do that as well as act as a trade union. No, I prefer to act as a trade union and deal with the Council as employers regardless of the task.'

In any case NALGO shared the manual unions' experience of changing management attitudes and resistance to informality. An additional obstacle to union-party linkages was thought by several NALGO officials to be Labour members' reluctance to recognise NALGO as a 'real' trade union since it was not affiliated to the Labour Party and was composed of 'middle class bureaucrats'. Insofar, too, as the unions insist on increased formalisation as a protection against employer inroads, they can hardly at the same time resort to informality when it appears expedient.

The diffusion of power within the majority group also creates problems for union negotiatiors where management negotiators lack authority and managerial authority is fragmented and uncertain. Labton illustrates the problems that arise from politically constrained management negotiators. The unions in Labton were very well aware that the job of personnel chair was a political hot potato and saw this as contributing to their negotiating difficulties:

There was also a tendency to put someone on the right of the Group in the Chair because it was thought that they would be more likely to take a stronger stand with the unions but it also meant that they were more likely to lack confidence in the negotiations. It's a bit like getting Ulster in the Cabinet, it was not something you agreed to but rather something you had thrust upon you.

Another union official linked the problem to the identity problems faced by Labour councillors as employers: 'in a Labour authority the weakness is that nobody wants to be in the position of an employer negotiating with a trade union'. Politically constrained chairs or just personally weak chairs can seriously impair employer-union communications, conveying a mistaken impression of employer intentions to a union with potentially major consequences. For example a former Labton NALGO official observed that the Union had at times formed the impression that the employer was refusing to make concessions and so the Union prepared for industrial action only to find that the Labour Group had been quite ready to make satisfactory concessions all along.

Conversely the centralisation of power within the ruling party decreases the opportunities for union negotiators to open up informal, alternative points of negotiation. Centralisation is a necessary (but not sufficient) condition for authoritative management negotiators. Of course the centralisation of political power in itself does not guarantee that a particular management negotiator has sufficient authority. The negotiators have to have sufficient personal influence to commit their group. Even in Conborough, an example of a politically highly centralised authority, one Chair of Personnel did not have the personal confidence nor the political weight within the Group to negotiate authoritatively. The unions had problems with this Chair as one former NALGO official observed:

He was a joke, whenever you tried negotiating with him all he would say was 'I have no mandate'. And I would say, 'Go and get a mandate, what's the point of you coming along here as Chairman if you have to keep running back to the Leader to check that it's OK'. And so much so that one day [we] burst into [the Leader's] room one day and said to him, 'You must get him off this Chair because he is useless – he's wasting our time, he's wasting your time, he's wasting everybody's time. He'll not negotiate on anything because he says that he can't.'

A personnel chair who can only act as a delegate of the majority group impedes effective negotiation. Union negotiators in Conborough and Labton expressed their preference for management negotiators who could act with relative independence and sell agreements back to their political colleagues. Their experience too was that it was easier for both sides to share important confidences with powerful rather than weak negotiators. Such an approach on the part of personnel chairs was greatly valued by the union leaders as enabling the maintenance of workable management-union relationships even in an authority as polarised as Conborough. One NALGO official in Conborough remarked on how he had valued the frankness of the first Personnel Chair:

> He negotiated very seriously, he used to say to us, quite honestly around the negotiating table, 'My Group wants you to achieve that, I'm telling you that's what I want you to go and achieve.' Then, if we reached an impasse, he would say, 'I understand what you're saying, I'll go back to my Group and tell them how far you're prepared to go', and if he had to concede or was sold by our arguments he would say, 'I can't say at this moment that I'll be able to get agreement from my Group but I'll go back and persuade them or argue with them' and eight times out of ten he would do that.

Elected and appointed management

There was a strong expectation among the staff and unions that the managerial role of the elected members should be relatively detached or independent of the officer management. In other words an expectation that the ruling politicians would not simply back up the appointed management regardless but make their own judgement about the rights and wrongs of a particular case. In the last chapter this relative independence of the elected members was seen as providing some useful flexibility for the management side, though significant differences in view between union and management over what is or is not an independent role can arise.

The elected members do have a formal arbitrating role as a court of appeal on disciplinary matters, permanent members of staff having a right of appeal over disciplinary matters to a sub-committee of the personnel committee in most authorities. Again even in an authority as polarised as Conborough, NALGO gave credit to an otherwise tough personnel chair for acting in a way independent of officer management over individual grievances: 'If he believes that they have been badly dealt with he will say that they have been unfairly dealt with and we will be asked to leave the room and the employing director stays behind and gets a rocket'. This NALGO official added that she could not have the same confidence in the Leader of the Council.

Thus industrial relations problems can arise from elected member failure to keep to an independent role. In Labton the union side saw some of their industrial relations problems as arising from such failures to maintain an independent role on disciplinary and similar matters. In the union view the most dramatic example was provided by the immediate events leading up to the Jones strike. The then NALGO leaders believed that the Personnel and Direct Works Chairs had simply backed up the officer management without attempting to make any independent judgement on the case:

I think decisions were made by officers which, if the members of the Council had been, if you like, quicker to stand back from and use their position to adjudicate from a distance and be objective about it, then the whole action could have been avoided. However they didn't do that, they leapt in to support their officers without examining the details of the case. In consequence we got into a situation of confrontation which neither side could retreat from, which was why we insisted that the inquiry was done from without the Council because by that stage they were all involved in backing the decision to keep him sacked and denying the allegations that we were making about them breaking agreements.

It should be added that, in retrospect, they also realised that they had almost forced the Chairs into backing the officer management by adopting an aggressive stance so early in the dispute. The Union side, of course, had believed that the situation was more urgent than in fact it was.

Departmental and personnel managers

Union leaders have to take into account not only the division between elected and appointed management but also that between the departmental and the central personnel managers. Taking departmental managers first, the union officials' relationships with them vary widely from department to department even in the same authority. One significant influence on approaches to the management side is the Union leadership's perception of the policy stance of a chief officer. Where chief officers are known to be opposed to retrenchment and sympathetic to the union position, the relationship can be quite close. A Conborough NALGO official described how one trusted chief officer had interceded with the Union for one of his colleagues who had been caught between staff taking industrial action and his Chair demanding a belligerent management response:

> We were in the Swan and the Director of . . . and Director of . . . were there, Jim came across and said, 'For Christ's sake can you get George off the hook?' We said 'yes' and spent the whole day cobbling together a form of words in his office which satisfied all sides.

This example illustrates a further point: that unions and senior management can have an identity of interest in steering potentially explosive issues away from members and resolving them between themselves. Unions and chief officers conspire together in this way where they fear that member involvement is likely to make conflict resolution more difficult. In Conborough the unions and some chief officers shared the concern that many Conservative members were becoming too keen on confrontation even where conciliation was very likely to lead to the resolution of a dispute. However this 'buffering' role of chief officers was declining as departing chief officers were replaced by officers less sympathetic to the unions. Moreover union relations with the chief officers believed to support retrenchment are likely to be distant with the unions likely to try to take issues to personnel. Equally union leaders' perception of a chief officer's style shapes their approach to departmental management. They are likely to try to circumvent those whose style is seen as authoritarian or unsympathetic, looking to direct contact with elected members or to central personnel.

Central personnel officers, then, are seen as alternative points of contact by union officials. The expectation, in both Conbrough and Labton, was that the central personnel officers should be independent of the departmental management over disciplinary matters and during disputes. Union officials felt freer to discuss problems with personnel officers whom they regarded as capable of independent judgement despite service department or even elected member pressures. The usual convention in local authorities, among management and unions, is that specifically departmental issues should be dealt with at departmental level (possibly at the departmental consultative committee), while issues with authority-wide implications require the involvement of the central personnel department (and possibly the joint consultative committee). Of course this distinction is often hard to sustain in practice especially in territorially minded service departments.

Nevertheless central personnel departments can form buffers between the ruling Group and the unions, as one Labton union leader recognised:

> Personnel is part of an overall management tool whereby you blunt the edge of the trade unions by taking the pressure off the other services . . . and you hand out little nuggets rather than proper gold. They are prepared to talk but invariably say 'no'. . . . the approach is relatively unsophisticated,you know, 'We'll absorb the pressure' rather than deal realistically with what we are saying.

It is not always easy for the unions to respect a hierarchy of management roles either within the officer hierarchy or between the officer and the elected management. For the most part union officials deal with the senior departmental management and senior personnel department officers rather than workplace management. Workplace managers, as distinct from the more senior departmental managers, often have great difficulty in coping with the problems arising from the increased tensions in the management–staff relationship and seldom have much experience of or training in industrial relations. The actions of lower management were a major source of industrial relations problems in Labton. In particular the immediate reasons for the Jones dispute arose in part from the actions of the local management in the Direct Works Department (though such a flare-up was almost inevitable given the growing management–union tensions in Labton). The unions detected a similar unwillingness to observe centrally agreed procedures in the running of certain residential establishments in the authority. Under these sorts of circumstances union officials felt bound to take the dispute away from the local workplace management as soon as possible.

Managing discontent

The task of leading local union organisations has grown in complexity and difficulty over recent years in terms both of welding together the leadership factions and mobilising the wider membership. Union leaders have to maintain a leadership base during a time when there are major organisational and ideological shifts towards democratisation and decentralisation – most notably through the introduction of shop steward systems. In addition the external pressures on unions are increasing factionalisation. The search for an agreed middle path between too much opposition and too much collaboration with the employer produces factions within the union leaderships (as was stressed in Chapter 3). The growth of factionalisation is further compounded by activists' involvement in the political debates arising from fiscal pressures and the ideological resurgence. An important consequence of these changes is the need for much greater political skill and sensitivity on the part of local union leaders.

Leading the local union organisation

One problem is that of sustaining effective leadership in the face of increased diffusion or decentralisation of power within the local union organisation. To manage discontent effectively requires some concentration of power in the hands of the leaders. Union leaders without power in their own organisations are severly disadvantaged in any negotiations with the employer in much the same way that personnel chairs without authority are in their party group. Effective negotiation requires authoritative negotiators on both sides.

Thus union leaders have to balance participative or democratic aims against the pragmatic aims of union effectiveness. The Conborough and Labton NALGO Branches offer an instructive contrast in terms of the management of industrial conflict. The Conborough NALGO leadership had the will and the political capacity within the Branch to fix a strategy and devise the appropriate industrial tactics assisted by the presence of a very real threat from the employer. They consciously tried to centralise power, finding that the pay-off ensured rank and file acceptance: 'we were totally Stalinist and undemocratic, some people [in the Union] used to criticise but as long as you were winning you got away with it'. Early on they decided that their only chance of resisting the employer was to acquire the powers to act independently and without constant reference back to the executive or membership, while the stewards became primarily a means through which grassroots membership could be mobilised. They tightly controlled the timing, extent and nature of the industrial action undertaken by the Branch and their use of selective action was an especially effective tactic.

In contrast successive Labton NALGO Branch leaders were constrained by the political instability of the Branch and by their own attachment to democratic and participative aims. Unlike Conborough they did not have the political advantage of a clearcut and major threat from the employers. Ideologically they saw themselves less as leaders and more as delegates answerable to the wider membership through the shop steward system and the Branch Executive. In consequence the use of industrial action by NALGO in Labton was poorly planned – during the Jones dispute the leadership exercised little strategic control over the development of the industrial action, but rather reacted to events with the result that they found themselves leading major strike action out of all proportion to the actual dispute. Such a reactive rather than anticipative leadership stance largely ruled out the use of selective action in a graduated way during that dispute.

The problem facing union leaders in an authority like Labton is more ambiguous than that facing union leaders in cutback authorities, though involving similar issues relating to the proper role of a trade union. One aspect of the problem is a tension between political ideology and pragmatism. Internal union debates between collaborationists and oppositionists are typically couched in both ideological and pragmatic or instrumental terms – ideologically the debates are about the desirability of a proposed initiative and instrumentally about what can be got out of any employer promoted change for the membership. For instance in Labton some union officials saw the decentralisation issue as one about increasing organisational responsiveness, while others saw it as an issue that primarily raised questions of conditions of service.

The evidence of Labton and other studies indicates that pragmatic considerations override the wider considerations. However, well-intentioned the employer might appear, union leaderships continued to see the role of the union as that of extracting the maximum advantage from the employer and not as smoothing the way for employer initiated change. This apparently widely accepted adversarialism prescribes the role of a union as being in permanent opposition to the employer. Even in Labour authorities where ideological and organisational affinities imply union cooperation with the employer, the reality is that union leaders remain strongly attached to an adversarial role.

Mobilising the rank and file

Another major problem in the management of discontent is that of mobilising the rank-and-file membership. One of the greatest inhibitions on union leaderships is the willingness of the membership to take industrial action. Thus the choice of union strategy is to a great extent based on those issues over which the leadership believes the members can be mobilised. It is very difficult to mobilise members over issues that are seen as having little bearing on their immediate economic interests even those such as the maintenance of existing levels of employment in the organisation. Threats to job security and to pay levels are the bottom line for union members. When these issues are seen to be at stake the leadership experiences few problems in mobilising the membership. As one Conborough NALGO official wearily observed, perhaps with some exaggeration:

> you know you can do anything to a NALGO member, you can cut his pay and cut his leave, you can screw him into the ground but compulsory redundancy they will fight to the death over. It's a simple fact of life that any white collar union has to face in the public sector – people have always come into local government not expecting high pay, not expecting marvellous conditions, the one thing they do expect is security of employment.

Most of the Conborough NALGO leaders believed that their priority had to be the defence of their existing members rather than that of some broader social objective despite national Union policy and the views of the oppositionists in the Union Executive: 'now it's an argument over the function of a trade union – is it our function to be concerned about the wider social issues of job loss . . . when we are faced by the responsibility of how we are going to protect ourselves and our people from compulsory redundancy? It's quite a decision to take.' The policy of the Branch, implicitly at least, was to cooperate with those cuts in exchange for guarantees of job security for Union members: 'We've cooperated with the cuts, with the job loss, and in return our members got security of job and many of them got higher grades.'

Problems of membership mobilisation also arise in determining the response of the local union organisations to policy innovation. The situation posed by policy innovation is more ambiguous than that posed by cutbacks not only for union leaderships but also for the union members. The views of the latter on policy innovations are typically more unformed or confused and conflicting compared, say, with the views of union members in a retrenching authority. Under these circumstances the problems faced by leaders in representing members' views and in forming a strategy are further compounded.

One aspect of this problem is coping with the conflicting expectations of the membership. Some members may look to the union to resist what they see as personally disruptive change and expect some compensatory concessions from the employer. Other members may expect the union to support the employers over policies they see as politically or professionally desirable or to press the employer for modifications to a new policy. Yet others may look to the union leadership for guidance on how to respond to proposed changes.

These varying expectations create difficult dilemmas for union leaders. One way of managing these conflicting expectations is for leaders to insist on defining the problem of policy change simply in terms of service conditions. Such a definition lessens the risk of the leaders becoming identified with one faction of the affected staff rather than another over the desirability or otherwise of a change. It is also politically safer for the leaders to adopt an adversarial stance over change as there is real leadership concern that too much cooperation with the political masters in policy change can provoke a membership revolt. These factors go a long way towards explaining the difficulties that many authorities like Labton have experienced in introducing policy innovations.

Relating to other unions

Local authority employees are not a homogeneous workforce but are divided by function and union membership. These divisions reduce the chances of united industrial action across an authority's workforce and pose a major problem of management for the various union leaders. The relationship between white collar supervisors and blue collar workers is one continual source of conflict and a major obstacle to inter-union cooperation; such difficulties arose in both Conborough and Labton.

Inter-union cooperation can be encouraged by the existence of a powerful threat to jobs through cuts and privatisation. In Conborough most manual union leaders recognised that they required the support of NALGO to increase the effectiveness of their strike action given the high substitutability of manual workers. While the NALGO leadership thought that the best strategy for the protection of their own members' interests lay in defeating any privatisation initiatives before they began directly to affect NALGO members. In the event inter-union cooperation had some success in raising the costs to the Council of retrenchment and privatisation. But there remained difficulties as, for example, when the NALGO leadership found themselves having to follow the manual unions' lead when the dustmen elected on strike action early in the refuse privatisation dispute.

In the absence of such a threat, inter-union cooperation is more difficult. In Labton there was a short lived Joint Union Campaign Against the Cuts set up after the Conservatives came to power in 1979, which faded out when the cuts over the first two years of Conservative Government proved to be less severe than anticipated (particularly in Labton where the Council absorbed the loss in central grant). The campaign against rate-capping was more loosely organised, the separate unions making their own campaigns. These difficulties of inter-union cooperation arose from a history of demarcation disputes between the main manual unions, illustrating one important problem that can arise from the multi-union nature of local government. In the late 1970s the local TGWU Branch recruited a large number of NUPE members who had become disillusioned with the competence of their local NUPE leadership, NUPE had seen this as an infringement of the TUC Bridlington Agreement and had resisted demands by the enlarged TGWU for parity of representation on the Joint Works Committee. Subsequently the TGWU had boycotted the Committee for two years until early 1984.

In addition tensions between white and blue collar staff are common. In Labton there were serious difficulties in the relationship between the manual unions and NALGO, difficulties which partly reflected differences in worldviews, as one NALGO official noted:

NALGO, being a white collar union, adopts policies like those of the Labour Party – it has policies on CND, on gays, women and blacks which NUPE gropes towards and unions like the General and Municipal are back in the Dark Ages. There is a classic story about the G and M. At one of the consultative committees in London where the NALGO Branch came forward and made a statement about gays, saying that one in twelve of the Council's employees were gay. And the G and M people there said that that might apply to NALGO members but does not apply to our members. That typifies the problems that NALGO has with the other trade unions.

More significant were resentments arising from the white collar supervision of manual workers. Much of this resentment centred on the Direct Works Department where the manual workers blamed the officer management for the Department's financial problems. In their turn the managers in that Department blamed the attitude of the craft unions. There was also a view within NALGO, not entirely unjustified, that other workers (especially the craft workers) had an inside track with the Labour Group: 'Direct Works is the classic example of always being told that we have consultative rights but when it comes to it it has already been stitched up in the Labour Club in Labton with the UCATT Convener and NUPE Committee.' Many of these resentments surfaced during the Jones dispute – for example the craft workers refused to be associated with the strike action.

Forming other alliances

The unions can strengthen their bargaining position not just through inter-union alliances but also through alliances with political factions on the council and with local user or consumer groups. Alliances with political factions can be important in keeping unions informed of management views during disputes and bringing pressure to bear on management negotiators. In Labour authorities, like Labton, the growth of factionalisation has increased the opportunities for forming such alliances. However in Labton union officials came to attach little importance to such alliances, even seeing some disadvantages: 'If you look to individual members to intervene on something, out of their ignorance they very often make a real mess out of it for you.' Another official added: 'we sometimes give them information but there's no way that we as a trade union could effectively service councillors to represent our arguments in the same way that the service management do for a Chair. I don't think that would be a good thing anyway.' In any case the Labton unionists were experiencing a growing Labour Group cohesion resistant to the type of covert negotiating approaches which had occurred during the Porters' Dispute.

Similarly the Conborough unionists had concluded that contacts with the opposition Labour Group were of little value. The unionists were actually better informed than the Labour Group partly because the Conservatives severely controlled the flow of information to the Labour Opposition and partly because the unions had a good disclosure of information agreement with the Council plus less formal sources of information. The unionists also found the Labour councillors unwilling to back them up over the privatisation dispute in terms of promises to revoke any privatisation if they came to office.

Alliances with local user or consumer groups are a relatively new development. Such alliances generally reflect a recognition both of a potential coincidence of long term interests between unionists and consumers (of the sort suggested by the fiscal crisis thesis) but more usually reflect a recognition of the immediate tactical advantages of coooperation. Such a developed example of such union-consumer alliances is instanced by the alliance between NALGO and local tenants associations in Conborough. While that alliance was successful in preventing the Council from going ahead with its immediate action (the feasibility study of housing privatisation), the unions and tenants failed to persuade the Council to negotiate over their proposals for reforming the housing service. But the absence of such developed alliances in Labton suggest that a shared and immediate external threat is a necessary precondition for the formation of alliances.

8 Managing under Pressure

Introduction

Public service organisations have been undergoing a major transition from being 'model' employers, setting an example to the private sector, towards being 'marketplace' employers. This transition, which is still in process, reflects the impact of major political and economic changes across the Western world. In Britain the transition is being engineered by the Thatcher Conservative Government which is intent on reforming a public sector seen as a haven of inefficient labour market practices. The Government has endeavoured to introduce competition and labour flexibility into the public sector. Local authorities have been especially affected by this new approach. Local authority pay, in common with the rest of the public sector, is now fixed on the basis of that sector's 'ability to pay' rather than 'comparability' with the private sector. Furthermore local authorities have had to adjust to severe reductions in central grant and successive measures intended to compel them to privatise services.

Continuing political trends mean that public employers are unlikely to return to their earlier role as 'model' employers within the foreseeable future. In Britain the Thatcher Government has been elected for a third term in office with a renewed commitment to rein in public expenditure and promote privatisation. Even in countries, like Australia and New Zealand, where labour parties are in power, growing concern with public expenditure has meant that they are increasingly coming into conflict with their public sector unions.

Public employers are becoming increasingly concerned with both financial and social control. They are now willing to risk stability and order in their organisations in order to strengthen their control over policy and work practices. Indeed they no longer have the financial resources available to provide incentives for employees to cooperate with the employer. Consequently the earlier relationship of corporatist harmony between public employers and employees is fading.

The aim of this book has been to understand the new problems facing both the policy makers as management and local union leaders. The employers, the elected politicians and senior officer managers, have been seen to be facing crises of management authority as staff and unions are now less compliant and more likely to contest authority; while the union leaders have been seen as facing their own problems of leadership in terms of managing discontent.

The focus has been on how the participants themselves are coming to terms with the new realities of industrial relations. The aim has been to give an analytical understanding of these realities to inform the real world practice of industrial relations. This practice has been introduced in the form of the types of options or choices available to practitioners. As the most effective way of demonstrating such choices is through actual examples, case studies have been used as the basis for a wide-ranging analysis of the problems of management and union leadership. The two contrasting case studies selected highlight the types of problems and choices facing managements and unions as the public sector faces growing fiscal pressures. They are typical inner city local authorities though they should not be taken as representative of British local government as a whole.

The analysis of the new realities of industrial relations has centred on three main questions. The first question asks how are the participants adjusting to the new pressures arising within the environment of their local authorities, particularly fiscal pressures from central government? The second question is whether the negotiability of change can be maintained and how, especially as policy change is now increasingly contested between management and unions? The third question is how do management and union differentiate management roles in industrial relations negotiations and in day-to-day management, especially as these roles and responsibilities have become contested and difficult to define? This concluding chapter reviews the findings of the book, focusing on the last two questions, and returns to the issues raised in the Introduction and Chapter 1 regarding the role of unions in public service organisations.

The negotiability of change: policy versus trust

The reformist and pluralist assumption underlying this study is that both sides have a strong and mutual interest in avoiding an all out power struggle. Accordingly the central problem of management has been seen as that of coping with the tension between policy and trust. Managements have been seen as having to reconcile two types of broad aim – the attainment of certain policy objectives (reflecting changes in their values or adjustments to a changing environment) and the maintenance of trusting relationships with the union leaders. This tension was fairly easy to resolve as long as three major underlying conditions pertained: that there was a strong normative consensus between management and unions; that the problems of political instability remained of little significance; and that the institutionalised consultative machinery functioned to facilitate the attainment of management aims.

Growth sustained these conditions of consensus and political stability. Over the years of post-war growth the increment of growth was used to accommodate policy change and to sustain a corporatist relationship. As long as change meant additions to the organisation rather than the switching around of existing resources, little opposition or conflict was aroused among staff and unions. The chances of opposition were reduced through the funding of incentives – in the form of enhanced career prospects, regradings and so on – to staff and unions to agree to policy change. Thus the availability of material incentives underpinned a high trust management-staff relationship and a relative absence of conflict across local government.

The fiscal crisis has reduced this former high degree of compatibility between policy change and trusting management-staff relationships. Conflicts over resources and the loss of incentives to staff compliance have increased the disruptive potential of policy change. Fiscal austerity also involves new political uncertainties over future expenditure and priorities, especially where management responses to the tightening of central government financial control have grown more uncertain. Consequently many managements are finding the traditional and formerly dominant strategies of cooptation and collaboration to be unworkable and turn to the newer strategies of conciliation and confrontation.

Local union leaders have a comparable concern with trust. They are confronted with the increasingly difficult problem of finding a middle way between trusting the management too much and trusting them too little. To trust the management too much is to risk losing too much control in favour of the latter, whereas to trust the management too little is to risk losing opportunities to influence and form understandings with the management. In other words the union leaders have to avoid, on one hand too much collaboration with the management and, on the other, too much confrontation. The increased significance of this search means that union leaders can be more vulnerable to leadership coups within their local union organisations. For other activists have greater scope to condemn existing leadership strategies as collaboration with and 'sell-outs' to management or alternatively as counterproductive confrontations with the employer.

Managing policy change

Policy change, whether in the form of retrenchment or innovation, creates tensions which reduce the workability of collaboration and cooptation as management strategies. Retrenchment policies, particularly when they threaten jobs, erode the normative consensus necessary to sustain these strategies. Thus policies of retrenchment are usually associated with the less consensual management strategies of conciliation and confrontation. Similarly innovative policies under financial austerity can also create industrial tensions that raise questions about the continued feasibility of collaboration and cooptation.

The critical question is how and to what extent can industrial tensions arising from policy change be managed? This question has to be answered by looking at the structure of power on both sides and the institutions of industrial relations, both of which have acquired great significance as the normative consensus between management and unions has weakened.

Firstly political leaders face new and difficult problems of control where the structure of power in their party groups is diffuse rather than concentrated. For the authority of the leaders, particularly their ability to negotiate authoritatively, is seriously compromised. Similarly union leaders have to be capable of concentrating power into their own hands if they are to negotiate effectively. If lead negotiators on either side lack the requisite authority to negotiate effectively, the whole process of negotiation will lose credibility and levels of mutual trust will be diminished. Moreover some degree of power centralisation is necessary if the institutions of industrial relations are to work.

Secondly in the face of growing tensions the institutionalisation of industrial relations contains conflict and, therefore, contributes to trust. Both management and unions rely on formal institutions and procedures to stabilise their relationship and maintain organisational order in the face of the forces of power diffusion. They have a strong mutual interest in maintaining organisational order as both are likely to lose if organisational chaos breaks out and undermines mutual trust. In addition management and union negotiators have a strong interest in institutionalisation which tends to bolster their leadership roles in their home organisations. Indeed the trend in local government has been towards increased formalisation and away from informality.

Significantly the scope of bargaining in local authorities is limited by their highly institutionalised decision making structures (as distinct from institutionalised industrial relations). The effect is to segregate 'political' or policy decisions from 'administrative' decisions which include industrial matters. Thus the scope of industrial negotiation is limited to the *process* of introducing policy change, while decisions on the *outcome* or substance of policy change tend to be excluded. For example institutionalised decision making removes sensitive decisions on retrenchment from the joint consultative machinery and, therefore from the normal channels of union influence. Union attempts to challenge certain decisions taken within the institutionalised decision making process can be ruled out of order or presented as challenges to the legitimate democratic process by employers. Meanwhile the unions are barred by institutional barriers and by considerations of political legitimacy from bringing such decisions into the scope of bargaining.

The paradoxes of employee participation and management authority

For a conciliatory strategy to work a considerable concentration of power is required within the home organisation (the party and the local union) as well as an acceptance of the institutions of industrial relations. Furthermore within a conciliatory strategy management has the further choice of a participative or authoritarian approach. A participative approach reflects the view that the best way to manage change is to encourage involvement by those affected. However managements face the *paradox of employee participation:* that opening up involvement in the process of planning change to those affected not only creates the possibility of greater cooperation from the latter, but also encourages opposition and increases the opposition's effectiveness.[1] Managements have also to respect due process to preserve trust despite the costs of institutionalised industrial relations in limiting their control and slowing down decision making. This paradox is a major reason why retrenching managements often resort to across-the-board cuts that aim to limit internal conflict through an equal allocation of misery.

Innovating managements may try to overcome the participation paradox at least initially by trying to coopt the unions by persuading them of the need for change. Such an approach has its limits as austerity conditions mean that the unions are reluctant to be coopted and see any proposed changes as scarce opportunities to extract concessions from the employers. The identity problem as employers faced by many Labour members also compounds the paradox. They expect to translate their relationship with the unions from a collaborative to a cooptative basis (as in Labton), assuming that the ideological and organisational affinities between the Labour Party and the unions mean that the unions should collaborate with management. Consequently they find it both difficult to understand and frustrating when the unions respond to policy change by bargaining even to the point where it seems that the unions are actually subverting Council policy.

The difficulties with participative approaches encourage managements to turn to more authoritarian approaches, especially once the industrial relations institutions come to be seen as major brakes on change. Labour as well as Conservative councillors increasingly have occasion to insist on their rights as the elected and legitimate decison makers. Again there is a paradox, this time the *paradox of managerial authority:* although management may have all the formal power that does not mean that they can achieve all their objectives. The exercise of authority under all circumstances is self-defeating as it tends to undermine consent among the workforce, instead managements have to win and maintain consent as well as issue commands. Indeed conciliation to be effective requires managements to share some control with the unions despite the limitations on management authority.

An important aspect of this dilemma of how far to share control is the sharing of information. Conciliation only works where management shares information with the unions (or is seen by the latter to do so). The continued concealment of information by management about their plans contributes to breakdowns in the formal consultative machinery and weakens mutual trust. For example in Conborough major departmental reorganisations, like that of the Housing Department, were sprung on the unions without prior consultation. In consequence the serious disputes following the announcement of the management's plans were resolved only after both sides resorted to confrontational stances outside the established disputes machinery.

The critical skills of political and indeed officer management lie in their abilities to resolve these paradoxes of employee participation and of managerial authority. They have to learn to accept the inevitability of resistance and how to cope with it, in particular finding a balance between revealing and concealing information as employer failure to share information is a major reason for lowered trust. In any case consulting with staff can assist management to avoid mistakes by checking proposals with those most involved.

Unions and policy change

The unions have a predominantly reactive rather than proactive role in relation to policy change. Nevertheless policy change, whether it be in the form of retrenchment or innovation under austerity, raises new and difficult questions of union strategy. Even when the unions become more reliant on conciliation as a strategy, they continue to face the difficult problem of finding a middle way between too much confrontation and too much collaboration. Outright resistance or confrontation may simply lead management to impose council policy on the staff regardless; whereas collaboration with the employers is more and more likely to seem a sell-out both to them and to competing leadership factions within the local union.

The formal industrial relations institutions can constitute a significant defence against employer promoted change, especially where those institutions still reflect the union gains of the years of growth. Formal agreements and procedures are important resources for the unions in resisting attempts by employers to increase their flexibility, whether it be flexibility in negotiations or in the management and deployment of staff. Certainly formal procedures can be used to slow down the rate of change and to open up at least some issues for negotiation. Union leaders faced by an innovating authority can insist on a narrow scope of bargaining, only negotiating over the service conditions implications of proposed changes and refusing to discuss the substance with management.

The effectiveness of the union leadership in negotiations over policy change depends not just on the presence of an institutionalised management–union relationship, but also on the power base of the leadership. Where that power base is weak the union leaders face difficulties in negotiating effectively with management, for they quickly lose credibility with management negotiators if they cannot negotiate without continual reference back to their union organisation or back up any threats of sanctions against the employer.

Policy innovation under austerity poses particularly difficult dilemmas for union leaders. Unions can seize the opportunity to extract concessions from the employer in exchange for compliance. When unions have otherwise few opportunities to make gains from the employer, they typically resist attempts by management to coopt them. Under austerity conditions policy innovation can also be a threat, particularly when there are considerable uncertainties over the future funding of local government. Major initiatives with considerable resource implications, like the decentralisation of services, are seen by many union activists as distractions at a time when jobs are under very real threat.

Any resort to confrontation and the use of threats of industrial action are high risk union strategies. The skill of successful union leadership lies in using threats of action but seldom having to carry out those threats. Even so leaders cannot issue threats unless they are confident of their ability to mobilise key groups of workers and manage the subsequent discontent. Key workers are those who occupy strategic locations in the organisation or have low substitutability or both (see Chapters 2 and 7). However strategic location and substitutability depend to a considerable extent on the politicians' perceptions of what is or is not a vital service that ought to be maintained if at all possible. For example historically the refuse collectors were a powerful group but they have lost power with the greater willingness of council employers to sit out strikes and bring in contract labour as well as with other factors such as rising unemployment.

Union members, especially white collar unionists, are not easily mobilised given their reluctance to lose income and risk disciplinary action from the employer. Accordingly the management of discontent requires careful judgements about when to call for action, particularly as calls to industrial action lose their urgency and potency if repeated too often. The evidence of Conborough indicates that even well-organised and strong union leaderships cannot successfully mount sustained campaigns of opposition, at least to an authority intent on service cutbacks. Meanwhile the Labton case illustrates how union leaders with a weak power base can lose significant credibility among their rank-and-file membership by failing to manage industrial action, as occurred after Jones' dismissal.

The limitations of industrial action may be overcome by forming alliances with consumer or user groups, as the Conborough unions did with tenants associations. These alliances can be effective in the short term, though they appear to be temporary and tactical in nature and do not involve the long term recognition of shared interests envisaged by O'Connor.[2]

Finally in the management of discontent union leaders have to cope with a *paradox of democratic leadership*. The recent trend has been to democratise unions through the introduction of new systems of workplace representatives and many local union leaders are committed to open decision-making. However the commitment to open debate within union organisations and the increased emphasis on majority mandates for action means that union leaders have their hands tied in managing expressions of discontent and in reaching compromises with management.

There is a last and important point to be made about the current leadership of many NALGO branches. The type of white collar militant leadership illustrated in this study may well be a generational phenomenon. The NALGO leaderships in both authorities appear to have brought value orientations to the workplace that were formed outside the employing organisation (see the social action approach). These 'educated radicals' or 'class of '68', as several of them referred to themselves, are likely to be the product of a particular period. Subsequent generations of officer may well bring a different orientation to work which will yet again change the union approach to industrial relations.

From fragmented to differentiated management

Fragmented management has been a long standing feature of local government. Financial austerity and increased political instability mean that the problems created by blurred and ill-defined managerial roles and responsibilities are no longer of minor importance. Managerial authority is now frequently contested both at the levels of member–officer relations and of management–staff relations. The responses to the consequent crises of management authority have involved a search for a proper differentiation of and definition of negotiating and management roles.

The perceived loss of management control by the political leaders reflects their inability to concentrate the necessary degree of power in their hands and, then, to formalise negotiating and management roles. Unless the leaders can marshall sufficient political support within their own party, their ability to control the organisation and act as authoritative negotiators will be limited by the diffusion of power. In particular they will be unable to contain the proliferation of informal points of negotiation, a development that threatens good working industrial relations. They will also be unable to use formalised industrial relations roles to bolster their authority as negotiators.

Meanwhile industrial relations have become too important to leave to the management officers, given the increased chances of industrial disorder and the greater political stakes involved. In many authorities the elected members are doubtful about the management officers' ability to contain that conflict especially after disputes like the Jones dispute at Labton. Such member doubts as well as uncertain political guidance (reflecting political instability) remove the ability of officers to negotiate authoritatively. Thus the officer managers tend themselves to withdraw from negotiating roles which they find difficult to carry out in favour of the elected members. Consequently the elected members are further drawn in to act as fully fledged industrial relations negotiators.

Politicians as negotiators

Even those elected members designated as management negotiators are unlikely to be able to negotiate authoritatively without a secure power base within their party. The skill of effective management negotiators (usually the personnel chairs) lies in their ability to stitch up agreements which they are confident are acceptable to their party group or which they can sell back to the group. However they are much more likely to be able to negotiate freely and authoritatively where power in the party group is concentrated and stable than where power is diffuse and unstable. Significantly even union negotiators complained about management negotiators in Conborough and Labton who were unable to negotiate effectively and were too politically constrained. Designated negotiators experience particular difficulties in Labour authorities where informal negotiating points arise from the ideological and organisational affinities between Labour members and the wider Labour Movement. Such political limitations on designated negotiators are sometimes present in Conservative authorities, usually in authorities, unlike Conborough, characterised by factionalism which weakens the authority of negotiators.

Even the most skilled political leaders face considerable difficulties in overcoming the destabilising effects of power diffusion. However there are group learning effects which over time can counteract the forces tending to power diffusion. The group experience of sharing the same problems and the same 'enemies' – whether they be central government, the chief officers' management team, NALGO or whatever – is important in producing group cohesion. Similarly the members of a party group often learn over time that management fragmentation (that is poorly differentiated management roles), for example, can have heavy costs when fragmentation contributes to the spread of industrial disruption or frustrates the resolution of disputes. They come to realise that giving the designated negotiators greater authority makes political sense. The Labton Labour Group illustrates such a learning process, Group members realised the value of properly differentiating roles and gave the Personnel Chair adequate authority and latitude. Other factors can also concentrate power, for example personal charisma can still be an important resource even in these highly ideological times.

Of course while concentrating power and authority into the hands of the designated negotiators is a necessary condition for the assertion of management control, it is not sufficient. A parallel process is also required whereby the political leaders institutionalise their authority through the formalisation and proper differentiation of management roles and responsibilities. This increased institutionalisation draws the line at the use of informal negotiating points and of backdoor influence, while that line is backed up by the political authority of the leadership. In this way the institutionalisation of industrial relations contains wider political forces as a necessary part of containing industrial tensions.[3]

The professionalisation of the personnel function is one significant form of institutionalisation. Strengthened personnel departments can have two major functions, as in the new and enlarged Labton Personnel Department. One function is the more obvious one of reinforcing the formal channels and providing the organisational means more effectively to monitor and police developments around the authority. Another function is that of an organisational buffer between the ruling politicians and the union activists to absorb pressures from the latter at a time when resource constraints mean that the former are less and less able to make concessions to the unions (that is shifting from a collaborative to a conciliatory strategy).

The unions as well as management have an interest in maintaining organisational order. Confusion can easily arise where union negotiators lack adequate authority or a power base within their home organisation. Thus they have to consider the dangers of disorder arising from the use of informal points of negotiation by other union activists and even themselves. While informality is quite compatible with collaborative or cooptative relationships between the two sides, it is less compatible with conciliatory or confrontational relationships. Nevertheless it must be stressed that informal discussions still have an essential role but only insofar as they complement the formal points of negotiation and take place between designated negotiators.

Politicians as managers

The elected members are increasingly drawn not only into industrial negotiations but also into the management of departments. Where they are committed to major policy changes, they grow impatient when the organisational machine is unable or apparently unwilling to deliver these changes. One source of this perceived organisational failure is often identified by them as laying in senior officers' inability or unwillingness to adapt to new political directions. The consequent search for new ways of tightening member control over the organisation leads almost inevitably to the appropriation of management functions formerly the prerogative of officer management. Such a tightening of control is particularly pronounced in authorities, like Conborough, where a political commitment to rapid retrenchment tends to create a distrust of officer management commitment to the politicians' goals. Such distrust leads the political leadership to take over key management tasks directly related to retrenchment, especially decisions on filling vacancies and on the review and organisation of departments. This concern to tighten political control extends to authorities innovating under austerity like Labton.

The close involvement of elected members in management raises further problems particularly in terms of the consistency of management policy. The elected members cannot be held accountable for their actions in terms of bureaucratic rules in the same way that the officer managers can. They are part-time politicians who are less bound by organisational precedent and previous agreements than officer managers and so are more susceptible to pressures leading to capricious decision-making and political patronage. This susceptibility has been seized on by some commentators as an argument for strengthening the role of officer management and removing councillors from day-to-day management decisions such as the disciplining and appointment of all but the most senior staff.

Of course given the now considerable importance of industrial relations in local government, it is inevitable and perhaps desirable

that the elected members should take the lead in industrial negotiations. However the case for member involvement in more day-
to-day management matters is not as strong. The paradox of
managerial authority applies to the member officer-relationship
as well as to the employer-employee relationship. The leading
members often find it difficult to reconcile their policy objectives,
or at least their selected means of achieving them, with the objective of 'letting the managers manage'. In Conborough the
Conservatives clearly cherished the latter objective yet their
concern with expenditure levels led their Staff Review Team to
insist on reviewing every proposed staff change.

As the paradox of management authority implies, such close
member involvement can impede the effective management of
the organisation as well as demoralise the officer managers. The
resolution to the paradox may be to impose national codes of
conduct on the member-officer relationship as has been argued
by the Widdicombe Report and others.[4] However while it is
important to differentiate roles, it is quite another thing to codify
those roles. The major difficulty with a national or even local
codification is that such a code will inevitably fail to take into
account the fact that role boundaries differ over time, among
authorities, among types of department and among personalities.
Moreover the process of forming relationships is at least as
important as the forms themselves. Consequently the aim should
be to create structures within which both sides can negotiate
over conflicts rather than impose unenforceable boundaries on
participants' actions. Nevertheless the problems that arise from
the discontinuity of the employer in a democratic institution, like
a local authority, should not be forgotten. While the administration (the ruling party or faction) may change, an incoming
administration inherits at least some of the employment responsibilities of their predecessor. They cannot simply discard previous
agreements with the unions nor reach new agreements without
considering the implications for future administrations.

Reclaiming the rights of management?

Crises of management authority have arisen as the control of
work has become increasingly disputed in local authorities. The

employers, elected members and senior officers, have been concerned with reclaiming what they perceive as the control over work practices lost to many white collar and blue collar local government workers during the period of post-war growth. In other words there has been a growing stress on the 'rights' of management and 'letting the managers manage'.

At the national level this new stress on the rights of the public employer has involved government questioning of collective bargaining in the public sector. In Britain the Thatcher Government now appears prepared to impose public sector pay settlements and even to abolish existing national collective bargaining structures. The prime example of this change in approach to public sector industrial relations has been the abolition of the Burnham Committees in education, with their local authority representatives, in favour of direct central government-union negotiations and the imposition of settlements on the teachers as happened in 1987. As yet the Government has continued to work with the existing Whitley system in other areas of local government pay but it has increased informal pressures on the employer side.

Some commentators have advocated dismantling the national Whitley system in favour of more localised bargaining in the public sector. The intention would be to move local authorities further towards being employers in the 'marketplace'. The argument is that local authorities should be able to employ people at the rate for the job in the local labour market and not be compelled to pay at national wage settlement levels. Those authorities in low wage areas would be able to reduce their staff costs, while those in high wage areas would be able to overcome recruiting difficulties by offering higher remuneration. The local government unions are opposed to local bargaining which they see not only as seriously reducing their members' incomes in low wage areas but also as severely weakening unionism across local government.

Another way of strengthening the 'rights' of management is to place legal limits on trade unions and industrial action. Indeed the Thatcher Government has already introduced major legal limits on union organisation and action covering both the private and the public sectors in the 1980 and 1982 Employment Acts and the 1984 Trade Union Act. Under these acts to avoid possible court action a strike must involve a 'trade dispute' with the employer, must not involve mass picketing or secondary picketing by sympathetic members of other unions, and have been authorised by a secret ballot of all members. In addition unions now can only establish or maintain political funds and Labour Party affiliation if a majority of their members vote in support in an individual ballot every ten years. How successful these legislative changes have been in weakening the unions is unclear as unemployment seems likely to have been at least as significant in reducing union membership and overall strike levels in Britain.

In addition to these measures, which apply to the private as well as the public sector, some commentators have advocated further restrictions on industrial action in 'essential public services'. The argument is the same as that used by pluralists like Wellington and Winter that the unions have excessive power because of their supposed monopoly power in these essential services.[5] Accordingly this monopoly power can be broken by legal limitations on the use of industrial action. However the US experience with legal restrictions on strike action suggests that these restrictions have not significantly affected strike levels.[6] Of course the majority of strikes are short-lived and the employers are often reluctant to apply legal sanctions and worsen even further their relationships with the workforce. Furthermore unions can resort to action short of strikes so that any legislation would have to define a large category of prohibited activities if it were to achieve its aims. In any case much research throws into question the view that industrial conflict is necessarily undesirable.[7] To try to prevent the expression of conflict through strike action may simply mean that such conflict is expressed in terms of falling morale, the departure of key staff and rising levels of absenteeism or even sabotage.

Yet another way of reinforcing management control is through competitive tendering and privatisation. The employer can compel its direct workforce to adopt new work practices and relinquish control over work by obtaining tenders from private organisations. This process of 'tender testing' existing in-house provision enables the ever-present threat of privatisation to be used to encourage staff and unions to keep costs down. Meanwhile privatisation itself can be used to reclaim management control and reduce costs. Local authorities themselves have to abide by the rules and service condition of the public service, including union recognition and staff consultation. However privatisation means that workers can be employed at local market rates and on less advantageous service conditions, while the unions can be circumvented and previous work practices revised. Indeed it is clear that the greatest savings from privatisation result from reductions in the wage bill (as both sides recognised in Conborough). Significantly privatisation in local government has been almost solely restricted to blue collar and not white collar work.

The need for learning strategies

Confrontation and blanket insistence on the rights of management are not sustainable in the longer term. Social and political attitudes have changed and while it may not be possible (or even desirable) to return to corporatist harmony, a return to Victorian management styles is an even remoter possibility. The real problems confronting both managements, the members and senior management officers, and unions are those of learning how to build and maintain good working relationships. The importance of mutual trust has been stressed as have the choices, the dilemmas facing managements and unions and the types of skills required to cope with those choices and dilemmas. The hope is that this book will assist this search for new ways of working with each other.

Guide to Further Reading

Industrial relations

There are a wide range of books available on industrial relations though unfortunately the literature on public service industrial relations is very limited. Michael Poole's *Theories of Trade Unionism: A Sociology of Industrial Relations* (London: Routledge & Kegan Paul, rev. ed. 1984). offers a detailed survey of the approaches sketched out in Chapter 1. Colin Crouch in his *Trade Unions: The Logic of Collective Action* (London: Fontana, 1982) gives a useful and stimulating framework for the analysis of union behaviour which was used in Chapter 3. John Purcell, *Good Industrial Relations: Theory and Practice* (London: Macmillan, 1981), is a valuable discussion of trust in industrial relations and of the ways in which trust develops between managements and unions.

A good introduction to 'new class' and 'proletarianisation' arguments can be found in the reader edited by Richard Hyman and Robert Price, *The New Working Class? White Collar Workers and Their Organisations* (London: Macmillan, 1983). Robert Price's introduction to theories of the growth of white collar unionism is particularly helpful. Nicholas Abercrombie and John Urry, *Capital, Labour and the Middle Classes* (London: Allen & Unwin, 1983) give a more detailed analysis of recent work on the middle class.

On corporatism and pluralism as political theories Reginald Harrison's *Pluralism and Corporatism* (London: Allen & Unwin, 1980) is a good introductory text. A more advanced account of corporatism can be found in Alan Cawson's *Corporatism and Political Theory* (Cambridge: Cambridge University Press, 1987). Finally A. G. Jordan and J. J. Richardson give a trenchant defence of pluralism in their *British Politics and the Policy Process* (London: Allen & Unwin, 1987).

Local government in Britain

The best general introductions to local politics in Britain are Gerry Stoker, *The Politics of Local Government* (London: Macmillan, 1988) and John Gyford, *Local Politics in Britain* (London: Croom Helm, 2nd edn, 1984). Other useful general books include Alan Alexander, *The Politics of Local Government in the United Kingdom* (London, Longman, 1982), and Martin Loughlin, M. David Gelfand and Ken Young, *Half a*

188

Century of Municipal Decline (London: Allen & Unwin, 1985). Martin Boddy and Colin Fudge (eds), *Local Socialism? Labour Councils and New Left Alternatives* (London: Macmillan, 1984), includes discussion of recent new left initiatives in local government.

The fiscal crisis

There are a large number of books on the fiscal crisis. The classic, of course, is James O'Connor, *The Fiscal Crisis of the State* (New York: St Martin's Press and London: Macmillan 1973). For a useful summary of the crisis and of recent changes to the financing of local government see K. Newton and T. J. Karran, *The Politics of Local Expenditure* (London: Macmillan, 1985). On cutback management Charles Levine (ed.), *Managing Fiscal Stress: The Crisis in the Public Sector* (Chatham N J: Chatham House, 1980) and L. Hirschhorn and Associates, *Cutting Back: Retrenchment and Redevelopment in Human and Community Services* (San Francisco: Jossey-Bass, 1983), offer some useful ideas, though mainly from the management perspective.

On privatisation the volume edited by Julian Le Grand and Ray Robinson, *Privatisation and the Welfare State* (London: Allen & Unwin, 1984), is a good introduction to the arguments.

Notes and References

1 Industrial Relations in Local Government

1. David Winchester, 'Industrial Relations in the Public Sector', in G. S. Bain (ed.), *Industrial Relations in Britain* (Oxford: Basil Blackwell, 1983) p. 155.
2. Richard Parry, 'Britain: Stable Aggregates, Changing Composition', in Richard Rose (ed.), *Public Employment in Western Nations* (Cambridge: Cambridge University Press, 1985) p. 79.
3. See, for example, A. L. Chickering (ed.), *Public Employee Unions: A Study of the Crisis in Public Sector Labour Relations* (Lexington: Lexington Books, 1976) and Mary Dickenson and Don Rawson, 'Trends in Public Sector Unionism', *Australian Journal of Public Administration*, 2, XLIV (June 1985) pp. 118–30.
4. This discussion is intended just as a basic introduction to the main theoretical debates, for a good, comprehensive survey of the differing authors see Michael Poole, *Theories of Trade Unionism* (London: Routledge & Kegan Paul, revised ed, 1984).
5. For a thorough analysis of the origins of pluralism in industrial relations see Richard Hyman, 'Pluralism, Procedural Consensus and Collective Bargaining', *British Journal of Industrial Relations*, 1, 16 (1978) pp. 16–40.
6. Quoted by Alan Fox, *Industrial Sociology and Industrial Relations*, Royal Commission on Trade Unions and Employers' Associations, Research Paper No 3 (London, HMSO, 1966) p. 4.
7. Alan Flanders, *Management and Unions: The Theory and Reform of Industrial Relations* (London: Faber, 1970) p. 86.
8. G. S. Bain and H. S. Clegg, 'A Strategy for Industrial Relations Research in Great Britain', *British Journal of Industrial Relations*, 1, 12 (1974) p. 95.
9. For an example of the pluralist approach see Robert A. Dahl, *Modern Political Analysis* (Englewood Cliffs: Prentice-Hall, second ed., 1970).
10. Alan Flanders, *Management and Unions: The Theory and Reform of Industrial Relations* (London: Faber, 1970) p. 205.
11. Royal Commission on Trade Unions and Employers' Associations, *Report*, Cmnd 3623 (London: HMSO, 1968).
12. The Whitley machinery will be described in more detail in Chapters 2 and 3.
13. Harry H. Wellington and Ralph K. Winter Jr., *The Unions and the Cities* (Washington, DC: The Brookings Institution, 1971).

14. Ibid., p. 61.
15. Ibid., p. 22.
16. Colin Crouch, *Trade Unions: The Logic of Collective Action* (London: Fontana, 1982) p. 104.
17. Though the Callaghan Labour Government lost the 1979 election at least in part as a result of trying to impose a 5 per cent pay norm on public service unions.
18. Terry Nichols Clark and Lorna Crowley Ferguson, *City Money – Political Processes, Fiscal Strain and Retrenchment* (New York: Columbia University Press, 1983) p. 171.
19. For example A. W. J. Thomson and P. B. Beaumont, *Public Sector Bargaining: A Study of Relative Gain* (Farnborough: Saxon House, 1978) p. 146.
20. Hugh Clegg, *Trade Unionism under Collective Bargaining: A Theory Based on Comparisons of Six Countries* (Oxford: Basil Blackwell, 1976).
21. Richard Hyman, *Industrial Relations: A Marxist Introduction* (London: Macmillan, 1972).
22. J. H. Goldthorpe, 'Industrial Relations in Britain: A Critique of Reformism', *Politics and Society*, 4 (1974) p. 442.
23. Hyman, *Industrial Relations*, p. 11.
24. For a trenchant defence of his position see Hugh Clegg, 'Pluralism in Industrial Relations', *British Journal of Industrial Relations*, 13, (1975), pp. 309–16.
25. Ibid.
26. For example one study of white collar unionism shows that the low level of white collar unionism is better explained in terms of the obstacles to union organisation rather than class and status, G. S. Bain, D. Coates and V. Ellis, *Social Stratification and Unionism* (London: Heinemann, 1973).
27. Hyman, *Industrial Relations*, p. 12.
28. John Purcell and Robin Smith, 'Introduction' in Purcell and Smith (ed.), *The Control of Work* (London: Macmillan, 1979) p. x.
29. John Purcell, *Good Industrial Relations in Theory and Practice* (London: Macmillan, 1981) and Alan Fox, *Beyond Contract: Work, Power and Trust Relations* (London: Faber, 1974). Although Fox's earlier writings seem to fall within the pluralist tradition, in *Beyond Contract* he developed a critique of pluralism from a social action perspective, emphasising the critical role of 'the mediating frames of reference, ideologies and aspirations' in work relationships.
30. Purcell, *Good Industrial Relations*, p. 53.
31. J. H. Goldthorpe, D. Lockwood, F. Bechofer and J. Platt, *The Affluent Worker: Industrial Attitudes and Behaviour* (Cambridge: Cambridge University Press, 1968) and *The Affluent Worker in the Class Structure* (Cambridge: Cambridge University Press, 1969).
32. Richard Hyman, *Strikes* (London: Fontana, 1972) p. 72.
33. For example Hyman, *Strikes*, p. 19.
34. Colin Crouch, 'The Changing Role of the State – Industrial

Relations in Western Europe' in C. Crouch and A. Pizzorno (ed.), *The Resurgence of Class Conflict in Western Europe Since 1968* (New York: Holmes & Meier, 1978) Vol. 2, pp. 197–220.

35. A good introduction to corporatism is Reginald J. Harrison, *Pluralism and Corporatism: The Political Evolution of modern Democracies* (London: Allen & Unwin, 1980); on a more advanced level Alan Cawson's, *Corporatism and Political Theory* (Oxford: Basil Blackwell, 1986) is especially good.
36. For a pluralist critique of corporatism see R. M. Martin, 'Pluralism and the New Corporatism', *Political Studies*, 1, 31 (March 1983) pp. 86–102.
37. Though see R. Rhodes, 'Corporatism, Pay Negotiation and Local Government', *Public Administration*, 3, 63 (Autumn 1985) pp. 287–307.
38. Cf. Thomson and Beaumont, *Public Sector Bargaining*, p. 157.
39. Ibid., p. 156.
40. Crouch, 'The Changing Role of the State', p. 216.
41. James O'Connor, *The Fiscal Crisis of the State* (New York: St Martin's Press, 1973).
42. Ibid., p. 249.
43. Ibid., p. 254.
44. Ibid., p. 249.
45. See Eric Lichten, *Class, Power and Austerity: The New York Fiscal Crisis* (South Hadley, Mass.: Bergin & Harvey, 1986).
46. Colin Crouch, *Trade Unions: The Logic of Collective Action* (London: Fontana, 1982) p. 39.
47. Ibid., p. 39.

2   Management Under Pressure

1. Notable exceptions are H. Mintzberg, *The Nature of Managerial Work* (New York: Harper & Row, 1973) and Richard E. Boyatzis, *The Competent Manager: A Model for Effective Performance* (New York: John Wiley, 1982). Unfortunately both books look at management in general and hardly deal with industrial relations.
2. Cf. S. Timperley, 'Organisational Strategies and Industrial Relations', *Industrial Relations Journal*, 2, (1980).
3. John Purcell, 'The Management of Industrial Relations in the Modern Corporation: An Agenda for Research', *British Journal of Industrial Relations*, 21, 1 (March 1983) p. 4.
4. Cf. Richard Rose: 'Political science studies have principally concentrated upon the ideas and institutions of "the profession of government", the recruitment of an administrative "elite", or the influence of "mandarins" upon high level policy. Concentrating upon a small fraction of the totality of public employees working for government risks, to paraphrase an expression, presenting the ghost without

Hamlet'. *Changes in Public Employment: A Multi-Dimensional Comparative Analysis* (Strathclyde: Studies in Public Policy No. 61, 1980), p. 3.

5. G. S. Bain, for example, considers favourable government attitudes to be the major explanatory factor in the development of white collar unionism, *The Growth of White Collar Unionism* (Oxford: Oxford University Press, 1970).

6. A. Strauss, L. Schatzman, D. Erlich, R. Bucher and M. Subshim, 'The Hospital and the Negotiated Order', in E. Freidson (ed.), *The Hospital in Modern Society* (London: Collier-Macmillan, 1963) and Anselm Strauss, *Negotiations: Value Contexts, Processes and Social Order* (London: Jossey-Bass, 1978).

7. For a description of the Burnham Committees see R. D. Coates, *Teachers' Unions and Interest Group Politics* (Cambridge: Cambridge University Press, 1972).

8. For a recent description of the workings of the Whitley system, especially the increasing interventions of central government, see R. A. W. Rhodes, *The National World of Local Government* (London: Allen & Unwin, 1986) ch. 5; and Kieron Walsh, 'Centralisation and Decentralisation in Local Government Bargaining', *Industrial Relations Journal*, 12 (1981) pp. 43–54.

9. Keith Thurley and Stephen Wood, 'Introduction' in their *Industrial Relations and Management Strategy* (Cambridge: Cambridge University Press, 1983) p. 3.

10. Thomas A. Kochan, 'A Theory of Multilateral Collective Bargaining in City Governments', *Industrial and Labour Relations Review*, 27, 4 (July 1974) pp. 525–42.

11. Michael J. Hill, *The Sociology of Public Administration* (London: Weidenfeld & Nicolson, 1972) Ch. 11; and George Jones, 'Varieties of Local Politics', *Local Government Studies*, 1, 2 (April 1975) p. 23.

12. For a study of these developments see Martin Laffin and Ken Young, 'The Changing Roles and Responsibilities of Local Authority Chief Officers', *Public Administration*, 1, 31 (Spring 1985) pp. 41–55.

13. For example John Gower Davies, *The Evangelistic Bureaucrat* (London: Tavistock 1972) and Norman Dennis, *People and Planning* (London: Faber, 1970).

14. The typical urban local authority in England and Wales, a metropolitan district or London borough, has the following main departments: finance, administration, personnel, social services, housing, planning, environmental health, engineering, recreation and (except London Boroughs in Inner London like Conborough and Labton) education.

15. For example T. R. Dye, *Politics, Economics and the Public* (Chicago: Rand McNally, 1966).

16. See John Dearlove, *The Politics of Policy in Local Government* (Cambridge: Cambridge University Press, 1973) pp. 61–70.

17. Cf. Dearlove, *The Politics of Policy* and Ken Young and Liz Mills, *Managing the Post-Industrial City* (London: Heinemann, 1983) pp. 6–24.

18. Ken Newton *et al.*, *Balancing the Books: The Financial Problems of Local Government in Western Europe* (London: Sage, 1980).

19. K. Newton and T. J. Karran, *The Politics of Local Expenditure* (London: Macmillan, 1985) p. 110.

20. For a good account of these recent developments see ibid., ch. 8.

21. Kieron Walsh, 'Centralisation and Decentralisation in Local Government Bargaining', *Industrial Relations Journal*, 12, 5 (1981) p. 47.

22. Dearlove, *The Politics of Policy*.

23. H. V. Wiseman's little monograph on Leeds City Council is the classic statement of this parliamentary view, *Local Government at Work* (London: Routledge & Kegan Paul, 1967).

24. C. Game and C. Skelcher, 'Manifestoes and other Manifestations of Local Party Politics', *Local Government Studies*, 9, 4 (1983) and C. Fudge, 'Winning an Election and Gaining Control: the Formulation and Implementation of a Local Political Manifesto', in S. Barrett and C. Fudge, (eds), *Policy and Action: Essays on the Implementation of Public Policy* (London: Methuen, 1981) pp. 123–142.

25. See Martin Boddy and Colin Fudge (eds), *Local Socialism? Labour Councils and New Left Alternatives* (London: Macmillan, 1984).

26. One of the leading proponents on the left of a 'rainbow coalition' is Ken Livingstone, the former Leader of the Greater London Council. See Tariq Ali and Ken Livingstone, *Who's Afraid of Margaret Thatcher?* (London: Verso, 1984). For a good survey of recent changes in the Labour Party see John Gyford, *Local Socialism* (London: Allen & Unwin, 1985).

27. For an important and telling study of these influences see Peter Saunders, *Urban Politics: A Sociological Interpretation* (Harmondsworth: Penguin, 1980).

28. These points will be explored further in the next chapter.

29. A. Strauss. L. Schatzman, D. Erlich, R. Bucher and M. Subshim, 'The Hospital and the Negotiated Order' in E. Freidson (ed.), *The Hospital in Modern Society* (London: Collier-Macmillan, 1963) p. 165.

30. John Purcell, *Good Industrial Relations: Theory and Practice* (London: Macmillan, 1981). This is a central argument of Purcell's book.

31. Ibid., especially chapter 8.

32. This formulation of the management problem was suggested by Hugh Heclo and Aron Wildavsky's summation of the underlying dilemma facing senior civil servants in the Whitehall 'village': 'There is no escaping the tension between policy and community, between adopting actions and maintaining relationships, between decision and cohesion, between governing now and preserving the possibility

of governing later. To cope with the world without destroying the understandings their common life requires – this is the underlying dilemma facing the community of political administrators.' *The Private Government of Public Money* (London: Macmillan, 1974) p. xv.

33. Cf. John Stewart, 'From Growth to Standstill' in Maurice Wright (ed.), *Public Spending Decisions: Growth and Restraint in the 1970s* (London: Allen & Unwin, 1983) pp. 9–24.
34. Thurley and Wood, *Industrial Relations and Management Strategy*, p. 198.
35. Phillip Selznick, *TVA and the Grassroots* (Berkeley: University of California Press, 1949) p. 13.

3   Unions Under Pressure

1. Colin Crouch, *Trade Unions: The Logic of Collective Action* (London: Fontana, 1982) p. 67.
2. Mancur Olson, *The Logic of Collective Action: Public Goods and the Theory of Groups* (Cambridge, Mass.: Harvard University Press, 1965).
3. Though this has not stopped strikes, see Martin Oppenheimer, *White Collar Politics* (New York: Monthly Review Press, 1985) p. 167. The Federal Government has generally been more sympathetic towards public service unions than state governments, but President Reagan's sacking of striking air traffic controllers in 1981 symbolises a new approach, ibid., p. 176.
4. For example see Alan Arthurs, 'GCHQ and the Changing Face of Staff Relations in the Civil Service', *Industrial Relations Journal*, 16, 2 (Summer 1985) pp. 26–33.
5. G. S. Bain and R. Price, 'Union Growth in Britain: Retrospect and Prospect', *British Journal of Industrial Relations*, 21, 1, (1980); and Mike Ingham, 'Industrial Relations in British Local Government', *Industrial Relations Journal*, 16, 1 (Spring 1985) p. 9. Ingham notes that the surprisingly higher figure for white collar unionisation may reflect the higher proportion of part-time workers in the manual workforce, part-time workers being less lightly to join unions.
6. Ingham, Ibid., p. 9.
7. Figures based on a survey of local authorities reported in Mike Ingham, 'Industrial Relations in British Local Government', p. 9.
8. The NUT has about 220 000 members; The National Association of Schoolmasters/Union of Women Teacher (120 000 members), the Assistant Masters and Mistresses Association (80 000) and the Professional Association of Teachers (23 000). Ken Jones, 'The National Union of Teachers', in Martin Lawn (ed.), *The Politics of Teacher Unionism* (Beckenham, Kent: Croom Helm, 1985) p. 287.

9. This paragraph is based on R. D. Coates, *Teachers' Unions and Interest Group Politics* (London: Cambridge University Press: 1972).

10. David Lockwood, *The Blackcoated Worker: A Study in Class Consciousness* (London: Allen & Unwin, 1958) p. 187.

11. Quoted in A. Spoor, *White Collar Union: Sixty Years of NALGO* (London: Heinemann, 1967) p. 47. This paragraph is based on Spoor's history of NALGO.

12. Despite having been formally registered as a union in 1920, A. Spoor, *White Collar*, p. 77.

13. Ken Prandy, 'Professional Associations in Great Britain', *Industrial Relations*, 5 (October 1965) p. 73.

14. Paul Blyton, Nigel Nicholson and Gill Ursell, 'Job, Status and White Collar Members' Union Activity', *Journal of Occupational Psychology*, 55 (1981) pp. 33–45.

15. Spoor, *White Collar Union*, pp. 80–97. In a similar vein William A. Robson wrote in the 1940s '[NALGO has] long been in the forefront of the movement for raising the educational standard of the clerical and administrative classes of the municipal civil service. Its efforts in this direction, made for the most part in the face of a blank wall of apathy and reactionary indifference manifested by local authorities, are highly credible and far-sighted.' *The Development of Local Government* (London: Allen & Unwin, 2nd edn, 1948) p. 300. The development of the local government professions exhibited a similar 'anti-localist' tendency, see Martin Laffin, *Professionalism and Policy: The Role of the Professions in the Central-Local Government Relationship* (Aldershot: Gower, 1986) esp. ch 3.

16. H. A. Clegg, *General Union: A Study of the National Union of General and Municipal Workers* (Oxford: Basil Blackwell, 1954) p. 1.

17. Richard Hyman, *The Workers' Union* (Oxford: Clarendon Press, 1970)

18. H. A. Clegg, Alan Fox and A. F. Thompson, *A History of British Trade Unions Since 1889*, Vol. I (Oxford: Clarendon Press, 1964) p. 88.

19. Gasworkers Annual Report quoted in Clegg *et al.*, *A History of British Trade Unions*, p. 88. Subsequent legislation has disallowed council employees from standing for election to their employing council.

20. For T&GWU and NUGMW membership figures see Clegg, *General Union*, p. 30.

21. David Lockwood, *The Blackcoated Worker:*, p. 140 and p. 187.

22. Ken Young, 'Re-Reading the Municipal Progress: A Crisis Revisited', in Martin Loughlin, M. David Gelfand and Ken Young (ed.), *Half a Century of Municipal Decline 1935–1985* (London: Allen & Unwin, 1985) pp. 1–25.

23. Quoted in P. B. Beaumont, *Government as Employer – Setting an Example* (London: Royal Institute of Public Administration, 1981) p. 14.

24. William A. Robson, *The Development of Local Government*, p. 322.
25. For a recent description of the workings of the Whitley system, especially central government interventions, see R. A. W. Rhodes, *The National World of Local Government* (London: Allen & Unwin, 1986) ch. 5.
26. Unfortunately statistics on industrial action in local government are not collected separately from those of the public sector as a whole. Figures are available between 1966 and 1975 which indicate an increasing incidence of strike activity but after that date there are no national figures available. For the 1966–75 figures see Kieron Walsh, 'Local Government militancy in Britain and the United States' *Local Government Studies* (November/December 1982) p. 6.
27. See D. Volker, 'NALGO's Affiliation to the TUC', *British Journal of Industrial Relations*, 4 (1966) pp. 69–76.
28. Spoor, *White Collar Union*, p. 529 and ch. 33 for an account of NALGO's entry into the TUC.
29. Undy *et al.*, *Change in Trade Unions*, p. 241.
30. Winchester, 'Industrial Relations in the Public Sector', p. 168.
31. The following table sums up the changing relationship between local government and private pay:

LOCAL GOVERNMENT/PRIVATE SECTOR PAY
1970–1986 (Private Sector = 100)

Year (April)	Males Manuals	Non-manuals	Females Manuals	Non-manuals
1970	81.9	101.1	94.1	163.8
1971	84.6	100.0	97.8	154.9
1972	84.5	106.0	98.8	161.2
1973	84.1	102.3	99.9	156.4
1974	84.4	102.2	101.4	150.6
1975	93.2	108.1	107.7	157.8
1976	92.0	112.2	102.8	162.5
1977	85.6	106.5	98.8	154.4
1978	86.3	99.8	95.7	146.5
1979	84.0	96.9	93.3	138.4
1980	91.3	98.1	97.6	135.8
1981	91.4	106.1	100.8	150.4
1982	87.3	102.2	100.5	141.5
1983	87.7	102.4	99.5	138.7
1984	85.6	98.1	99.1	132.5
1985	83.7	95.7	97.8	128.0
1986	83.4	94.0	99.2	128.9

N.B. As the non-manuals include the index-linked firemen and police as well as APT&C and teachers, the table exaggerates the position of local government white collar workers.

Source: Local Authorities Conditions of Service Advisory Board, *Manpower Digest*, no. 20, December 1986.

32. The actual figures are 512 160 in June 1975 to 379 054 in June 1986, a fall of 26 per cent in full-time manual employment. Because the level of part-time employment remained virtually the same over this period, the number of full-time equivalents fell by rather less, from 766 977 to 633 298, a fall of just over 17 per cent, (LACSAB, *Manpower Digest*, No. 22, February 1987).

33. *Manpower Digest*. The fall in numbers of teachers is mostly accounted for in terms of the effects of falling school rolls.

34. From 1967 to 1973 the average annual increase was 3.5 per cent, in 1974–75 it has been estimated at 3.3 per cent and in the following year at 5.8 per cent. Richard Parry, 'Britain: Stable Aggregates, Changing Composition', in Richard Rose (ed.), *Public Employment in Western Nations*, (Cambridge: Cambridge University Press, 1985) p. 74. Unfortunately no more detailed breakdowns into manual and non-manual categories are available before 1975 when the collection of manpower statistics for local government began in the 'Joint Manpower Watch'.

35. James O'Connor, *The Fiscal Crisis of The State* (London, Macmillan, 1973).

36. H. Braverman, *Labor and Monopoly Capital* (New York: Monthly Prsss, 1974.

37. David Winchester, 'Industrial Relations in the Public Sector', in George Sayers Bain (ed.), *Industrial Relations in Britain* (Oxford: Basil Blackwell, 1983) p. 165.

38. Martin Oppenheimer, 'The Proletarianisation of the Professional', in Paul Halmos (ed.), *Professionalisation and Social Change*, Sociological Review Monograph No. 20 pp. 213–28. For more recent statements of the thesis see the volume edited by Charles Derber, *Professionals as Workers: Mental Labor in Advanced Capitalism* (Boston: G. K. Hall, 1982).

39. Especially Daniel Bell, *The Coming of Post-Industrial Society* (New York: Basic Books, 1973) and *The Cultural Contradictions of Capitalism* (New York: Basic Books, 1976).

40. For the most recent statement of his position and criticism of the proletarianisation thesis see Eliot Freidson, *Professional Powers: A Study of the Institutionalisation of Formal Knowledge* (Chicago: University of Chicago Press, 1986) esp. chs. 6 and 8.

41. For example John Gower Davies, *The Evangelistic Bureaucrat* (London: Tavistock, 1972) and Norman Dennis, *People and Planning* (London, Faber, 1970).

42. Martin Laffin and Ken Young, 'The Changing Roles and Responsi-

bilities of Local Authority Chief Officers', *Public Administration* 1, 31 (Spring 1985) pp. 41–55.

43. Ibid.

44. Michael Lipsky, *Street-Level Bureaucracy: Dilemmas of the Individual in Public Services* (New York: Russell Sage Foundation, 1980). Lipsky defines 'street level bureaucrats' as 'public service workers who interact directly with citizens in the course of their jobs, and who have substantial discretion in their work' (*Street-Level Bureaucracy*, p. 3). Examples of street level bureaucrats include social workers, teachers, policemen, lower court judges, housing managers and environmental health officers.

45. See Undy *et al.*, *Change in Trade Unions*, p. 231. As was noted earlier these differentials appear to have widened again in the 1980s.

46. A. O. Hirschman, *Exit, Voice or Loyalty* (Cambridge, Mass. Harvard University Press, 1970).

47. Thus in their study of white collar workers in three organisations (including one local authority), Rosemary Crompton and Gareth Jones found that 'protection' emerged as a major reason for union membership among the NALGO members, *White-Collar Proletariat: Deskilling and Gender in Clerical Work* (London: Macmillan, 1984) p. 199.

48. Nigel Nicholson, Gill Ursell and Paul Blyton, *The Dynamics of White Collar Unionism: A Study of Local Union Participation* (London: Academic Press, 1981). p. 212.

49. R. Undy *et al.*, *Change in Trade Unions*, ch. 8.

50. Ibid., p. 293.

51. For a discussion of the introduction of a stewards system in NALGO see George Newman, *Path to Maturity: NALGO 1965–80* (Manchester: Cooperative Press, 1982) ch. 23.

52. For a study of the introduction of such a system in Sheffield see Nicholson *et al.*, *The Dynamics of White Collar Unionism*.

53. For a similar formulation of the problem see Charles Sabel, 'The Internal Politics of Trade Unions', in Suzanne D. Berger (ed.), *Organising Interests in Western Europe* (Cambridge: Cambridge University Press, 1981). p. 225–6.

54. See Eric Batstone, Ian Boraston and Stephen Frenkel, *The Social Organisation of Strikes* (Oxford: Blackwell, 1978) p. 28.

55. C. Wright Mills, *The New Men of Power* (New York: Harcourt Brace, 1948) p. 9.

56. Michael Mann, *Consciousness and Action Among the Western Working Class* (London: Macmillan, 1973) p. 49.

57. Paul Blyton, 'The Coexistence of Managers and Managed in a Single Trade Union Branch,' in M. Poole and R. Mansfield (eds), *Management Roles in Industrial Relations* (Aldershot: Gower, 1980) pp. 129–36.

8   Managing under Pressure

1. See also Charles H. Levine's discussion of a similar paradox, 'More on Cutback Management: Hard Questions for Hard Times' in Charles H. Levine (ed.), *Managing Fiscal Stress: The Crisis in the Public Sector* (Chatham N. J.: Chatham House, 1980) p. 308.
2. See Chapter 1 and James O'Connor, *The Fiscal Crisis of the State* (London: Macmillan, 1973) p. 254.
3. Compare John Purcell's description of 'the stepped sequence in conflict resolution' in *Good Industrial Relations: Theory and Practice* (London: Macmillan, 1981) p. 238.
4. The Committee of Inquiry into the Conduct of local Authority Business, *Report* (Widdicombe Committee) Cmnd 9797 (London: HMSO, 1986).
5. Harry. H. Wellington and Ralph K. Winter, *The Unions and the Cities* (Washington DC: The Brookings Institution, 1971) and see Chapter 1 of this book.
6. P. B. Beaumont, 'The Right to Strike in the Public Sector: The Issues and Evidence', *Public Administration Bulletin* no. 35 (April 1981); and Martin Oppenheimer, *White Collar Politics* (New York: Monthly Review Press, 1985) pp. 167–8.
7. See, for example, P. K. Edwards, 'Strikes and Unorganised Conflict: Some Further Consideration', *British Journal of Industrial Relations* 21 (June 1979) pp. 95–8; and P. K. Edwards and Hugh Scullion, *The Social Organisation of Industrial Conflict* (Oxford: Blackwell, 1982).

Index